Community

Community

DAVID WEISSMAN

SUNY PRESS

Cover Credit: Katherine B. Weissman

Published by State University of New York Press, Albany

© 2025 State University of New York

All rights reserved

Printed in the United States of America

No part of this book may be used or reproduced in any manner whatsoever without written permission. No part of this book may be stored in a retrieval system or transmitted in any form or by any means including electronic, electrostatic, magnetic tape, mechanical, photocopying, recording, or otherwise without the prior permission in writing of the publisher.

Links to third-party websites are provided as a convenience and for informational purposes only. They do not constitute an endorsement or an approval of any of the products, services, or opinions of the organization, companies, or individuals. SUNY Press bears no responsibility for the accuracy, legality, or content of a URL, the external website, or for that of subsequent websites.

For information, contact State University of New York Press, Albany, NY www.sunypress.edu

Library of Congress Cataloging-in-Publication Data

Name: Weissman, David, 1936– author.
Title: Community / David Weissman.
Description: Albany : State University of New York Press, [2025] | Includes
    bibliographical references and index.
Identifiers: LCCN 2024028133 | ISBN 9798855801040 (hardcover : alk. paper) |
    ISBN 9798855801057 (ebook) | ISBN 9798855801033 (pbk. : alk. paper)
Subjects: LCSH: Communities.
Classification: LCC HM756 .W45 2025 | DDC 307—dc23/eng/20241008
LC record available at https://lccn.loc.gov/2024028133

For Kathy
My wife, editor, and artist

Contents

Introduction	1
Chapter 1. Community	11
Chapter 2. Infrastructure	33
Chapter 3. Meaning and Normativity	55
Chapter 4. Autonomy	89
Chapter 5. Cooperation and Conflict	113
Chapter 6. The One and the Many	131
Afterword	147
Notes	149
Index	153

Introduction

The writing of *Community* was provoked by irresolution in a current debate. The side I prefer objects to the unqualified emphasis on freedom from interference and freedom to act in any way causing no harm to others (John Stuart Mill's no-harm principle[1]). Unfettered individualism is criticized by writers who object that individual freedom is constrained by a society's culture and laws, and by the family and education that shape one's talents and inclinations. But something is missing: many writers decry social atomism while failing to specify the social contexts where individuals are formed. Filling that gap is the aim of Amitai Etzioni, Philip Selznick, Robert Nisbet, and, less abstractly, Alasdair MacIntyre's *After Virtue*.[2] MacIntyre is more specific than the sociologists: they are generalists; he describes three social groups—the Amish, conservative Catholics, and orthodox Jews—as they sustain practices and personal identities appropriate to their history and ethos. His account fascinates readers while mystifying them: why celebrate traditional ways when many find them rigid and repressive? A dismissive response calls the groups tribal. I suggest that they are better described as communities, each with social, political, and economic interests specific to itself. MacIntyre has identified a key organizing factor in social life, yet his concern is the moral coherence of the communities he describes, not community structure or diversity. *Community* supplies a likely version of the missing account. It helps correct a lazy habit: we speak of socialization as if it implies immersion in vaguely specified societies, though it occurs as we acquire the habits, values, and tensions of distinctive families, schools, neighborhoods, and jobs.

Utilitarian communities are often vigorous because members can't neglect interests and tasks—infrastructure, schools, and hospitals—that won't be satisfied without organization and planning. Yet communities bound by meaning and feeling—families, friendships, and cultures—are fragile, though critical to social stability. Wealth and technology have made us independent and mutually remote; individualism has convinced us that communities are never more than loosely bound. Mill is emblematic: "(F)rom this liberty of each individual follows the liberty . . . of combination among individuals; freedom to unite for any purpose not involving harm to others."[3] Communities, he suggests, are aggregates—groups—having no functional or moral integrity apart from converging member interests. This ignores aims that aren't satisfied without stable communities or the coordination of those having complementary skills (such as farmers and those who transport their crops). People, he implies, are otherwise mutually indifferent; purpose or feeling isn't enough to bind them.

The result—social fragmentation and anomie—is a moral wound. Its deep cause is incompatibility in the styles of organization that compete within Western societies, both described by Ferdinand Tönnies in 1887. One, *gemeinschaft* (community), is holistic and prescriptive; the other, *gesellschaft* (society), is open, tolerant, and pragmatic. Society is a totalizing community dedicated to God or the Good; or its social space is morally and theologically neutral, open to all who respect Mill's no-harm principle. Gemeinschaft enforces its versions of community. Communities other than utilities are often loose or ephemeral in gesellschaft.

One may suppose that *community* is useful principally for evoking sentiment, occasions remembered or foreseen. Yet this sense misconstrues the power of the word and its referents. Communities are distinguished by their organization, interests, and aims. Every utilitarian community competes for space and resources; each is a locus (with agency) of political negotiation and economic calculation. There is more to say, because all communities, whether utilitarian or bound by meaning and feeling, are engines of socialization. Families, schools, neighborhoods, and jobs: learning what we say and how to

INTRODUCTION   3

say it; knowing what to want and how to get it, we learn how to be within them.

We emphasize communities because their aims and functions are critical to our welfare. Yet we abstract from their differences to emphasize the generic features distinguishing utilities (veterinarians and barber shops) from communities of meaning (friendships or religions). We track their movements and relations, like meteorologists tracking weather, while indifferent to their aims and effects. Or we distinguish among them—families from businesses and schools—in order that socially acceptable communities may secure themselves while pursuing their aims. We don't ask drivers where they're going or require that they explain their choice of companions; we don't choose their cars. We do regulate traffic flow. Tracking community structures and needs clarifies the miasma of affiliations and conflicts glossed as *society*.

The Uses of *Community*

One estimate alleges that the word *community* has ninety-four different uses.[4] Many are allusive, with only locale or a generic interest (talk of the Icelandic or dental community) giving them referents. The communities of my concern are collaborations that serve the needs of practical life. The three principal variations are communities-of-interest assembled for a task or because of a taste; communities-of-meaning that emerge when emotions or shared understandings establish mutual trust among people bound by an aim; and communities-at-large implying that all a society or people of a kind—members of a religion, race, or gender—assemble when something said or done provokes their pride or vulnerability. These are the stable entities of our social lives. We aren't surprised by families, businesses, and schools, though we are surprised by communities—flash mobs or a grateful audience—that electrify social relations when they emerge unpredictably. Stable communities are more easily regulated because their aims and needs are known; those occurring spontaneously—riots, for example—are harder to manage.

4 COMMUNITY

Disciplinary Social Spaces

Each community-of-accord is a disciplinary space prefigured by an ideology. What is good or bad, tolerated or reproved: these spaces are moral, conceptual backdrops for practices they sanction. Subaltern communities—communities-of-interest, -meaning, -spontaneities, or -at-large—form within them; people usually behave as required. Values are agreed because learned in childhood without discussion or explanation. Societies have one or more of these disciplinary frames, though having more than one invites conflict. That happens, for example, if the social space is ambiguous: one is free to choose a mate or vocation or choices are foreclosed because both are arranged by one's family. An open society's partisans would have us compare the energy levels within these versions of social coherence: one is holistic and inert, the other is diverse, mostly stable but inventive and usefully self-transforming. Authors described as *communitarian* favor this processive, democratic view.

> [C]ontemporary communities tend to be new communities that are part of a pluralistic web of communities. People are, at one and the same time, members of several communities, such as professional, residential, and others. They can, and do, use these multi-memberships . . . to protect themselves from excessive pressure by any one community.[5]
>
> It is not slipshod to speak of the European Economic Community, the Catholic community, the university community, the law school community or the police as an occupational community. The main point here is that a framework of shared beliefs, interests, and commitments unites a set of varied groups and activities. Some are central, others peripheral, but all are connected by bonds that establish a common faith or fate, a personal identity, a sense of belonging, and a supportive structure of activities and relationships.[6]

The "framework of shared beliefs, [and] interests" commits a society's members to an open playing field where all are free to participate in activities or aims consistent with Mill's no-harm principle. For there are many things to do and ways to be. Most require, to some degree, the support of others. We often construe our interdependence in terms of behavior or materiel because emotional bonds seem less vital: one can live without them, though Robert Nisbet emphasized "spontaneous associations"[7] and "psychological devotions"[8] because feeling seals community with unity and purpose.

Charles Taylor would have us assemble in this other way.

> One understanding of secularity . . . is in terms of public spaces. These have been allegedly emptied of God, or of any reference to ultimate reality. Or taken from another side, as we function within various spheres of activity—economic, political, cultural, educational, professional, recreational—the norms and principles we follow, the deliberations we engage in, generally don't refer us to God or to any religious beliefs; the considerations we act on are internal to the "rationality" of each sphere. . . . This is in striking contrast to earlier periods, when Christian faith laid down authoritative prescriptions, often through the mouths of the clergy, which could not be easily ignored in any of those domains.[9]

These conceptual alternatives—societies open to initiative and dissent versus those in thrall to a holistic religion or ideology—are mutually exclusive, though social practice profits from both. Totalizing designs promise fellowship, stability, and safety within a community of the whole, properties more attractive to many people than the open societies where communities are weak and commitment is ephemeral. Yet there are accommodations: holistic solutions are commonplace in laissez-faire societies where practical considerations—police, fire, and education—oblige members to qualify individual freedom in the name of public health. Solutions like these are welcomed, without reducing the contrariety of the two designs: one sanctions many communities and occasional holistic interventions in an open space; the other prefigures a community that punishes dissent, while fixing the beliefs and practices acceptable within its space. Both are communities-of-accord, meaning that participants affirm their society's dominant form: totalizing prescription or tolerant diversity.

Autonomy or Reciprocity

Many instrumental relationships verge on fellowship without achieving it because participants inhibit feelings that would transform fellow workers into something closer to friends. But sometimes utilities are remade as communities-of-meaning. Imagine Jack and Jill on a nervous first date: when do they become partners? What is the normative and emotional structure of the space their partnership creates? How does it shape action and feeling? How are they newly enabled, yet constrained by their duties to one another? Six related topics require more elaborate answers.

Stability. Loyalty to others, many barely known, doesn't seem noteworthy until one notices their absence. One misses the shop that closed. Relations were formal but cordial; one will duplicate the service, maybe not the feeling. Is there a structure common to every such relationship, those we extol as meaningful and those discounted as merely convenient? Surveying our roles, we discover the landscape of our reciprocities, some that are only instrumental, others infused with meaning and prized for their intensity. Holism's partisans say that efficiency is too great a cost for the mutual indifference and spiritual decay occurring when meaning yields to pluralism, opportunity, and calculation. But their idea of community is narrowly based on the control of people acceding to the routines and expectations of their church or regime. It fails to acknowledge that bonds of several kinds—ephemeral or enduring, emotional or conceptual—imbue lives with meaning in disciplinary spaces of both kinds, gesellschaft as well as gemeinschaft.

Autonomy or reciprocity. Ideas promoting community are often reactions to the social atomism implied by talk of autonomy and freedom. Mill's *On Liberty* supposes that choice has no limit but physical incapacity and the demand that we do no harm to others. But is this a sufficient basis for sociality, when nothing in his book directs the education of children or qualifies the objection that *On Liberty* is largely mute about the relations of adults? We require Mill's *Utilitarianism* for ideas about the effects of emotion and morality on choice amid complexity, competition, and conflict.[10] These books exhibit the tension generated by the opposing demands of social coherence and personal autonomy.

Which has priority, duty to a social system or the freedom to choose and pursue aims of one's own? Can we arrange—do we have—social systems in which duties to some are compatible with free choice? Is autonomy satisfied by performing social roles in ways appropriate to one's skills, temperament, and the expectations of others? Or does it require that we ignore duties and roles while going our separate ways? People assembled for a task feel the tension generated when individuality stymies collaboration. The choice is reminiscent of Plato's *Republic*: an autocrat prescribes a society's design and the relations of its members; or democracy requires that productive activity be left to individual choice and voluntary collaboration. Policy fills the space between these two: how much autonomy is permitted or encouraged; how much routine is required to satisfy basic needs? Efficacy and social cohesion is our vague but real middle ground. Duties may supersede autonomy; but should that happen always or often? The balance shifts with context: from holism to pragmatic pluralism, as one drives in traffic or orders lunch. Autonomy is the topic of chapter 4.

Aims and values. People responsible for a social system need information about its aims and values. Answers come with responses to questions about the system's formal and efficient causes: What is its design or what should it be? What are its members' energies and intentions? Is it a friendship, a business, or a nation? Answers vary with systems and their contexts, but also because of the properties distinguishing communities-of-meaning from relationships that are principally or only utilitarian: families from boarding schools. Utilities are designed for a task; people filling their roles are rewarded for efficiency, not for their cordiality, though social systems work better when mutuality softens instrumental relations. The first chapters consider these qualities and the difference they make.

Appeals to community. What is implied by the frequent uses of *community* in late-industrial societies where communities-of-meaning—families and friendships apart—are often rare? Is this a way of compensating for our emphatic individuality? Do we use the word *community* to evoke the sense of togetherness encouraged by societies dominated by religion or ideology, though absent in many lives? Are we grasping, like Heidegger, for the security and purity no longer assured in transactional societies where diversity, competition, and initiative are assumed? We may imagine living within the virtual reality prefigured by a story—winning a lottery with an imaginary ticket—but then we're demoralized when its number isn't called. Is this the anomie that explains our many appeals to community?

Schism. Societies fragmented by sects or tribes are described as *communitarian.* What are the acceptable strategies for public order and governance when tribal differences preclude accord? Public life in Canada tolerates the communal differences discouraged by French secularism, but what's to be done when tolerance and education fail to reduce sectarian violence? Is it acceptable for a state to reduce violence by defending the interests of one side while suppressing the other? My response is at best a clarification, not a solution.

The One and the many. A community's relation to its members, then a society's relation to its constituent social systems is the expression of an ancient metaphysical issue: the One and the many. *E pluribus unum* is a slogan signifying the unity of free men and women or the unity of a nation whose people emigrated from other places. What explains their unity? is it seamless or merely an aggregate honored with a word? This issue is fundamental to mereology (the study of the relation of parts to wholes), but its solutions are principally syntactic and logical. Alternative formulations explicate unity in terms that are more recognizably material: this essay emphasizes reciprocal causal relations as they bind individuals, communities of both kinds, and their networks. Two late chapters of John Dewey's *The Public and Its Problems*—"The Eclipse of the Public" and "Search for the Great Community"—seek a basis for community in America. What could it be, he thought, if not reverence for the rational principles making a common life viable, and respect for the fellow citizens with whom one shares its possibilities? Obstacles to that hope aren't resolved in any state larger than Finland or Denmark.

Negotiation and Calculation

Community formation, like the management of community relations, is fraught by political contention and the calculations of economic advantage. The weighing of cost and benefits is apparent in relationships as simple as friendship: What does the friend need? What do I need? How does this relationship impact others? How do I prioritize my various duties and inclinations in ways that reduce friction and costs while maximizing my advantage? Policies and practices are contentious because they affect other people or communities and their interests. Communities simplify negotiations because they consolidate the interests of many in the guise of One. These are the same calculation whether the domain is personal or an affair of state.

Community preferences and decisions are formulated by individuals in the light of personal experience and deliberation. Resolution comes at distinct orders: first within a community, then in its relation to others. Families negotiate with one another, Norway negotiates with Denmark, but their many respective members or citizens do not negotiate with one another. This discipline is, of course, ideal, but it's often breached by people or businesses that see an advantage to eluding it.

Other Sources

Aristotle remarked that humans are political animals.[11] Societies organized either way—whether totalizing or pluralistic—confirm that this is so, yet each accentuates past or present social systems without implying the process responsible for their generation. Social life is better understood and sometimes better controlled if we know the variables determining these outcomes and the values giving them force. Securing that more ample idea requires attention to each of the five issues above. Books addressing one or two of them are familiar. Alasdair MacIntyre's *After Virtue* celebrates the coherence of traditional cultures. Books by Charles Taylor, Ronald Dworkin, Michael Sandel, Will Kymlicka, and others emphasize libertarian excesses, while espousing laws and practices favorable to social goods. They agree that bonding is commonplace in nature though different among us because of habit, expectation, and partners' demands. Yet no formulation known to me considers these issues while providing an ontologically grounded account of the infrastructure enabling community formation. Sociality is not mysterious; it's autonomy that needs explaining in a world where individuality is emergent while reciprocity—entanglement—is the original social condition.

Semantics. communities-of-interest is used synonymously with *instrumentalities* and *utilities; communities-of-meaning; communities-at-large,* and *communities-of-social or -political accord* are used throughout as indicated above. *Community,* alone, signifies a community-of-meaning. The word *system(s),* and the phrase *social system(s),* are used to signify relationships of all four kinds. Systems are organizations or associations bound, as explicated in chapter 1, by the causal reciprocities of their parts. (The *systems* of my *A Social Ontology*[12] are this book's *communities.*) Exposition sharpens reference when these clarifications fail.

Chapter One

Community

Society

Society is community's context. I suggest that it be characterized as follows: people living together, under established laws in close quarters (or with ready electronic access), share meanings and practices refined by their history and circumstances. They establish webs of interdependence, expectation, and intention, while satisfying common needs and personal interests. Every society has momentum and diversity because of its communities-of-interest and -meaning. They cohere to some degree because each is regulated by a community-of-accord, a system of ideas and values that prescribe a people's beliefs and practices. Societies native to two or more communities-of-accord sometimes converge because principal values—safety, health, education, and productivity—are common to all; but there is also the risk of schism.

Communities-of-Interest and -Meaning

Communities provide efficacy, fellowship, safety, and warmth. What explains their coherence and our comfort? Affiliation is one attribute; confidence in the loyalty of one's partners is another. Yet one doesn't use evocative terms when describing relations to bank tellers or detectives: why use them here? Because they emphasize the difference between utilitarian relationships and those locating us within systems where efficiency is softened by empathy and trust.

The foci of utilitarian relationships are their tasks; focus within communities-of-meaning is an idealized aim (harmony or justice) or mutual care. Utilitarian relationships are vital to safety and well-being. Communities-of-meaning are something more: their significance in members' emotional lives is captured in a phrase—*being in a relation-ship*—a condition that valorizes a bond while making one responsible for actions due the other. Add reciprocity, and we have friendship: a community of two or more. Each is an agent affecting the other while acknowledging duties to him or her. Communities of both kinds vary through ranges of intensity: friendships that are warm or merely respectful, doctors one sees rarely.

Communities-of-interest evolve into communities-of-meaning when participation intensifies members' convictions or nourishes their skills. Church choirs and fan clubs embody utility and meaning: they express belief or a taste while organizing to promote it. Vocations are natural sites of community formation; their communities endure, because talent and education qualify members the work they do. A humdrum office job becomes one's entrée into meaning, as one befriends other workers or learns an organization's purpose and why it matters. But there is diversity in work and no simple paradigm for doing it. Team-mates play together, though painting, writing, composing, and design require agency—the independence and isolation that turns random ideas into order and relevance. Communities don't do these things, though individuals do them better when they are aware that their work is appraised and used.

Emotion is puzzling if we worry that anything epiphenome-nal—like the red glow of a wire heated by an electric current—lacks agency or depth. Yet fellow feeling or a shared religion or ideology are the binders distinguishing communities-of-meaning from utilitar-ian relationships. Creating them is a challenge in our transactional economies. One thinks of big cities where able people thrive amid an ethos that construes meaning as little more than tolerance for dif-ference. When do utilitarian collaborations stabilize as communities-

COMMUNITY

of-meaning? Transitions are fragile and hard to sustain when people bond principally or only to defend their interests, though friendship and marriage are familiar exceptions to our habits as loners. Residual communities-of-meaning—principally families, friendships, schools, and religious sanctuaries—are no less familiar, though pluralistic and local, than the totalizing communities of a church or regime.

Small social systems–of-utility or -meaning—are paradigms of coherence because their structure is apparent. All embody a geometry resembling a jigsaw puzzle: pieces fit the shapes of others in complementary ways. Each of a system's members—however many there are—has a role with three aspects: (1) each satisfies and sustains the relationship by requiting a duty to the system; (2) each calibrates his or her actions in ways appropriate to a task; and (3) each satisfies his or her partners by acting in ways that satisfy their expectations. These features are common to utilities (schools or stores) and to communities-of-meaning, though meaning adds a dimension absent in many utilities and mostly incidental to their function. For these are communities that prize fellowship in reciprocity; clumsiness can be excused but carelessness in respect to others cannot. This, its emotional bond and moral purpose, explains the coherence and vigor in a friendship.

There is also this ambiguity: saying that each of a system's partners acts as its role requires applies as much to ants and bees as to humans. We say that duty in those nonhuman beings lacks a moral dimension because it's hard-wired—automatic rather than willed. But duty in us is also satisfied thoughtlessly when responses are habitual because learned. What distinguishes us from them? They act (we suppose) without a motive; we're different because of sensibilities engaged as we satisfy our roles in ways responsive to partners, tasks, and duties. These relationships are closed circles: they exclude most other people and concerns. The sense of closure is incidental much of the time—when paying a bill, for example—though it has weight in relationships traditionally regarded as communal. We know who and where we are in families, neighborhoods, and religions where security and worth are the effects of fellow feeling and the specificity of one's partners: your friends rather than mine.

14 COMMUNITY

This is community as it locates us within circles of stability: some desirable, others not. Why stay in relationships that are punishing? Because people fear their vulnerability to alternatives that may be worse; and because the experience of suffering is often embedded, one may be unable to imagine a different self.

Communities-at-Large

Communities-at-large has meaning in two senses. One signifies all of a society's people as they live within a sovereign state while satisfying its laws and practices. (We speak derivatively of community property: streets, parks, and schools.) But *society* is vague: it implies aggregation, each person linked to some, while indifferent to most others. Describing a society as a community adds nuance: it implies a variable—fellow feeling, history, an interpretation (religion or ideology), history, culture, laws, or a productive economy—responsible for its coherence. The other sense is implicit when community is suppressed in people distinguished by belief or taste, or by ethnicity, race, or gender. These differences may be incidental and ignored, though community formation accelerates when members are aroused by grievance or pride, or when people of a kind are threatened or attacked. Perpetual discomfort is one of anxiety's effects; sectarian conflict is another.

Communities-at-large are a focus for the reverential idea that people are bound by blood, God's care, or republican values. Heidegger at one extreme, Dewey and Rousseau at the other, map some principal understandings of the people. Fascination with the rural *volk* is diminished by the multiculturalism flourishing in principal cities, and by the initiatives encouraged in competitive economies. The dream of pastoral fellowship isn't cogent in cities where personal or common interest outruns the fear of difference. Yet the fantasy is strong: it's unlikely that the promise of meaning—feeling or shared belief—should be the respected binder of small groups while never affecting people who bond willy-nilly to people mostly unknown.

Communities-of-interest and -meaning are typically substantial, visible, and active: the family next door, the barbershop nearby. They incite the pragmatic thinking responsible for laws governing commerce and everyday life. Communities-at-large—especially those established by allegiance to an ethnicity, race, or idea—often draw the lines of social fracture. We respond to something said or done when it seems to threaten safety or personal identity, hence the political conflicts they provoke. A tolerant society smooths fissures that would otherwise risk schism or civil war.

Spontaneity

Stable communities resemble familiar houses on an old street: there is nothing provocative about them. It's the spontaneous communities—celebrating crowds, some welcoming, others hostile—that are unsettling: do we join them, or keep our distance? The challenge ramifies with the complexity of a locale: are there many such communities or never more than a few? Big cities teach inhibition and patience: communities you join, others you tolerate or ignore as they pass.

Why use *community* when speaking of mobs or crowds? Because of their cohesion: they are energized and sustained by the reciprocal causal relations—the mirroring—of their members.

Being-in-the-Truth

Social systems are sustained by their effects—by their utility and/ or meaning. A job has meaning if it pays one's bills; friendship has meaning because it generates mutual loyalty and care. Yet people keep or change jobs for reasons that are only utilitarian; loyalty to communities-of-meaning is significance of a different order We know the difference because we're quick to reject the charge that allegiance to emotionally charged relationships—meaningful communities—is always motivated by an instrumental advantage.

The meaning of that kind has several aspects: it presupposes a condition valued for itself (not as means to something else), then adds these considerations: a strong and favorable emotional response, an idealized aim (happiness or salvation), and loyalty to a community's members. It may also be critical that meaning captures one's emotional and intellectual adherence to a tradition: I am one of them. This is the complex experience characterized as "being-in-the-truth." The experience of a community's significance—its idealization—is often membership's signature. Yet the ways of construing one's experience as a community member is not always transparent: one may be strongly moved without perceiving a community's purpose or the depth of one's commitment. Habit alone explains its effects in some members; others regard participation as the worthiest expression of their moral lives. All may share the persuasion that each has greater value because of the fellowship and purpose that come with membership. Every such point of reference makes empathy and affiliation, rather than utility, the basis for one's sense of identity: my communities—whatever their scale—make me recognizable to others while shaping behavior that makes me visible to myself. Utilities don't usually have this effect; many spend a lifetime working for a business without feeling defined by it.

Descartes affirmed that each thinker has an immediate self-perception.[1] But what is its content: do I perceive myself in the guise of a role or as a being among those who value one another irrespective of their roles? The answer is relevant to community because Descartes implied that what we do is incidental to self-discovery—me, thinking—except that a current activity is contingently its touchstone. The alternative affirms that one's role-defining tasks—those I think about and satisfy—are critical to identity, whether perceived by others or oneself. It may be true—I assume it—that both alternatives contribute to the sense of being a thinker, an agent, with an identity: I am self-perceiving, irrespective of my roles, but also self-identifying when perceiving the actions they require. These two are often or always joined, though their coupling concedes that identity depends, to some large degree, on having roles sanctioned by one's systems, whether communities or utilities.

Gemeinschaft and Gesellschaft

Communities of all these kinds form in a disciplinary space, a community-of-accord. Ferdinand Tönnies described two principal alternatives.

COMMUNITY 17

[T]he theory of *Gemeinschaft* starts from the assumption of perfect unity of human will as an original or natural condition which is preserved in spite of separation. This natural condition is found in manifold forms because of dependence on the nature of the relationship between individuals who are differently conditioned. The common root of this natural condition is the coherence of vegetative life through birth and the fact that the human wills, in so far as each one of these wills is related to a definite physical body, are and remain linked to each other by parental descent and by sex, or by necessity become so linked.[2]

Reciprocal, binding sentiment as a peculiar will of a *Gemeinschaft* we shall call understanding. It represents the special social force and sympathy which keeps human beings together as members of a totality.[3]

The theory of the *Gesellschaft* deals with the artificial construction of an aggregate of human beings which superficially resembles the *Gemeinschaft* in so far as the individuals live and dwell together peacefully. However, in the *Gemeinschaft* they remain essentially united in spite of all separating factors, whereas in the *Gesellschaft* they are essentially separated in spite of all uniting factors. So, in reality, something that has a common value does not exist.[4]

Philip Selznick explains, as follows:

Tönnies thought he could discern within each of his two types a basic way of thinking, feeling, and acting. The more primordial form he called Wesenwille, translated as "natural" or "essential" will.

Wesenwille, the basis of *Gemeinschaft*, expresses a condition or state of being rather than a set purpose. It is motivation or conduct that emerges from growth and adaptation, that is, from the accumulation of experiences

18   COMMUNITY

and commitments and from the formation of character; it
reveals a person's authentic self, which must be a product
of social history and social participation. A community
based on "natural will" is person-centered. Its institutions
recognize and uphold continuities of self and society.

Emotion, preference, and rationality are governed by
socially accepted criteria of intrinsic worth. The alternative
is Kurwille, the foundation of *Gesellschaft*. Kurwille connotes,
in Tönnies' usage, choice that is both rational and arbitrary.
In *Gesellschaft*, goals do not emerge from tradition or
from the fabric of social life; they are not expressions of
identity and self-conception. Rather, ends are forever posited
anew, in response to changing circumstances and desires, by
independent and rational actors. In this model the *choice*
of ends is arbitrary, but their pursuit is governed by
rational calculation. Thus *Gesellschaft* breeds a positivist,
utilitarian mentality. Within the framework, neither ends
nor means have intrinsic worth.[5]

Identity is simple in gemeinschaft because participants live in the
predictable ways of inherited beliefs and practices, though identity is
complex and precarious in gesellschaft, where agents integrate anomalous
roles in circumstances that aren't fully predictable or controlled. One
community, adapted to its people and circumstances, seems preferable
to a fragile mix of assemblies having no common aim. But unanimity
requires a social enforcer or a binding meaning. That condition is
probably unachievable in contemporary societies where traditional
authorities—church and state—have ruptured trajectories. No church
dominates economically prosperous states where reason, initiative, and
efficiency are acknowledged conditions for wealth, though gemeinschaft
survives in enclaves where, for example, churches celebrate the Latin
Mass. The counterforce is a granular array of communities varying in
scale and function. They emerge as autonomous agents form or inherit
systems that satisfy their emotional and motivational needs. Identity
is the complex of one's choices, not as before the life and manner
prescribed by a dominant community. Imagine the cognitive, moral,

COMMUNITY 19

and emotional ambience created by one's participation in a family or friendship.

Now suppose that all roles are stripped of meaning, then notice the emotional and moral void implied when every relationship has no significance apart from its mechanics, costs, or benefits.

Acknowledging gesellschaft averts the error that reserves talk of community to large-scale, holistic systems—typically religions and states—because smaller communities—families, congregations, businesses, or towns—are meaningful to their participants, though singular and local. Holism blinds us to the diversity of systems (whether communities-of-interest or -meaning) chosen or inherited, hence to the diversity of meanings and feelings propagated by the mix of autonomy and constraint: work or play; religion or politics. It obscures the contexts where children learn judgment and choice, each hard to learn because meanings and feelings diverge when discomfort fights duty. Those we can't integrate are shaded or abandoned; or we persist in relationships that make us uncomfortable because of loyalty, passion, or need. The coherence promised by gemeinschaft fractures for people living in gesellschaft societies when their systems, inherited or chosen, fail to integrate.

Dismayed by gemeinschaft's demise, wanting to find what's left of community, we look in the wrong places. Finding no compelling religious or ideological movements in principal cities and towns, we infer that community itself has died. We overlook the many communities formed when people establish productive or neighborly relations. It's quick but significant that one exchanges greetings every morning with a neighbor whose name one doesn't know, and that both would be annoyed if either were to ignore the other. This, too, is community, one defined by its stabilizing reciprocity and the duty each partner feels to the other. Now extrapolate from this example to the many, perhaps dozens of systems (communities-of-interest or -meaning) in which one is engaged, then consider that each person living in a society transformed by gesellschaft perceives him- or herself as the autonomous node, the agent of consequence, at the center of systems he or she has joined or formed. This, rather than the demise of community, is the inception of innumerable community fields, each the sustained creation of the willing agent at its center. Its granularity is the ensemble of his or her choices, the projection of his or her identity. Add that there are as many of these fields as there are autonomous agents abetted and sustained by the nurturing ecosystems where education, initiative, prudence, and luck enable some or many residents to make these choices. Subordinating communities—religions and ideologies—simplify members' lives by interpreting all or many activities in ways they prescribe: they tell us how to live. Compare city residents, each with an assortment of commitments, some that conflict, many that differ from those of neighbors or family members, each set too complex to represent with a simple formula. None can be unambiguously recommended because none is wholly desirable or intelligible, and none is known if one hasn't adjusted the mix of its parts while living within it.

Communities-of-Accord

Communities-of-accord are societies or constituent systems that have achieved consensus regarding principal moral and political issues. We distinguish accord in communities of two orders. The first comprises those who believe, in the spirit of Rousseau's *Social Contract*, that people living together can't live productively or survive their personal vulnerability without accepting rules and practices common to all. This is a community of moral and intellectual accord. Gemeinschaft and gesellschaft are its principal, more determinate lower-order expressions. Each has partisans who suppose that their version best expresses the higher order's values and demands, though accord is usually a consensus emerging over time as people enjoy an ethos they're never asked to explain or defend. Community, in this instance, is the in-gathering of those whose actions are calibrated to its forms of life: monogamy or polygamy, personal autonomy or priestly authority. Accord's second-order determinables—gemeinschaft and gesellschaft—are indifferent to the specificities of their lower-order expressions, yet the idea of disciplinary spaces generalizes to each of them. Every sphere in which we think ourselves free to behave in ways perceived as appropriate—families, businesses, schools, and teams—is

Community

a disciplinary space, a domain where choice is circumscribed by the duty to behave in ways it sanctions. Where friendship, home, school, citizenship, and work are disciplines, each of us lives in a complex of irregularly permissive spaces. Do anything you like appropriate to them, up to the point of harming others.

Several details that are material, though ancillary to distinctions they illustrate are discussed in the sections below.

Networks

Friendships seem free-standing, without commitments or duties to others; but many communities are multiply connected. Most utilities are linked to the several or many others from which they draw resources or to which they send a product or service. Communities-of-meaning are more often autonomous, though many—nuclear and extended families—are deeply nested. Coordination enables systems of both sorts to satisfy aims that are different, but complementary. Assembling these networks is settled in the societies of *gemeinschaft*, because they're prescribed: there are designs for the conduct of marriages, families, or schools, and designs for their links to one another. Almost every social act—marrying and raising children, for example—instantiates and reaffirms them. *Gesellschaft's* responses are less predictable: people may be quick to support a neighbor or relative, though they may feel no obligation to help if blood isn't thicker than water. That attitude isn't irrational in a disciplinary space where one's origin is less consequential for well-being than the shifting aims of one's allies.

Gemeinschaft makes its networks intrinsic to social design; its designs are rational in the way of ecclesiastical cities or Ebenezer Howard's *Garden Cities of To-morrow.*[6] Principal functions are emphasized; communication among them is assured; each is designed to affirm its aim. Gesellschaft's societies are inefficient by comparison, because, like vines, their growth is opportunistic. Car owners mated to their gas stations leave them for battery makers and electric chargers; change is quick because consumers are savvy. The effect is a Darwinian social landscape where loyalty to partners is often no more than a measure of perceived advantage.

Imagine the god's-eyeview from above a large city. Focus alters as the god blinks: it sees a milling aggregate, people going every which way for no reason it discerns, then a patchwork of clusters as people cohere. This isn't an omniscient god; it guesses and infers, as when looking for and seeing evidence that traces of affiliation bind clusters to one another. Which impression seems credible in reflection? Was there reality to the individuals of its first perception, or was their apparent autonomy the mistake of failing to discern the clusters to which they resolve? Were the clusters separable or merely distinguishable from others of their integrating networks? Are their networks separable or bound in subtle ways that elude a first impression? The decoherence of individuals and their systems seem confirmed: there is autonomy and agency. The pitcher isn't a shortstop, husbands aren't wives; but those are roles within relationships that are themselves systems within mutually implicating or impinging networks. How far up this scale does entanglement go before it implies a holism in which the decoherence responsible for individuality and separation struggles for breath? Hearts and brains are separate and different, though people having them are often sensibilize and intelligent because they share a language and disciplinary spaces.

Hierarchies

Gemeinschaft is essentially hierarchical: the whole prescribes conditions for the assembly of subaltern communities, whether families, schools, neighborhoods, governments, or parishes. Gesellschaft is hierarchical because the collaborations it incites often require an authority that regulates its people and systems. Neither space validates the nominalist belief that society is a flat array of loosely assembled individuals.

Essential Values

Why speak of gesellschaft's diverse relationships as *social systems*, *utilities*, or *instrumentalities*, thereby blunting the loss of attributes—meaning, feeling, and safety—that distinguish gemeinschaft? Because the distinctive properties of traditional communities often seem incidental to the utilitarian relationships dominating gesellschaft societies. Gemeinschaft favors global religions, regimes, or ideologies because of the sentiment and social control they afford: let authorities prescribe routines for all, with penalties for dissenters. Diversity, too, is powerful because it satisfies diverse inclinations, because its effects are unforeseeable, and because it frustrates or defeats authoritarian regimes. Yet gesellschaft is sometimes problematic: if friendship makes for community, so does a band of thieves. Acknowledging freedom and diversity, often encouraging them, we say that tolerance and discipline are its offsetting conditions.

What are community's values in an open society? Three are essential when it's assumed that utilities are embedded within communities-of-meaning: *tasks, responsible members* who freely choose or inherit and affirm roles pertinent to their tasks, and *meanings*—feelings, idealizations, loyalty, purpose, and trust—that create communities-of-meaning by binding their members.

A utility's *tasks* often make little or no claim to moral stature or to the emotional bonds of their participants. Communities-of-meaning do both. They satisfy their practical aims while swathed in the moral values of care and respect. Making us safe, comfortable, and effective, they help to make us good.

Responsible members inherit or choose their roles: gemeinschaft prescribes roles appropriate to tasks it considers appropriate. Women especially are assigned their tasks as managers of family life, though feminism is testimony to gesellschaft's emphasis on autonomy: do what you like or can within social spaces where talent and will, not gender, are the principal controls on one's choice of roles.

Meaning is emotional glue: it binds a community's members in fellowship and mutual loyalty. Cleaving to others, expecting the same of them, we feel an obligation without having to be told of laws or duties. Conventional laws are a goad to people slow to respond. Emotion and common understandings are a greater force: we're impelled to satisfy both personal inclinations and partners' expectations. Utilitarian relationships are instrumental; their moral implications are limited to the give and take of duty and reward. Emotion and fellowship enlarge the moral burden: cabs deliver passengers to their destinations; spouses and friends want more.

24   Community

These criteria apply to moral life in communities of all scales and intensities. Loyalties may be firm, though the strong intensities of friendship tail off to cordiality or respect among professional partners. Exceptions are apparent: there is little collaboration between parents and their newborn children, though the family bond is strong.

Diversity

The diversity of social systems, their actions and effects are clues that ordinary thinking about community is simplistic: Must systems be holistic or vital to spiritual health? Are deference and consensus sure signs of their worth? Systems we notice are far fewer than those we inhabit. Why so many? Because interests and needs oblige us to seek the help of many partners or the same ones in different roles. Bonding to them, we give loyalty or support for benefits received. Mill's third region of liberty characterizes these utilitarian systems. He doesn't tell us how people acquire the talent for working together, but there is an answer: would we bind ourselves to others if we hadn't recognized their skills and our needs while living as children in families, neighborhoods, or schools? Because, if so, we're unlikely to be remote from similar communities-of-interest or -meaning as adults.

What sorts of communities are those likely to have been? What is characteristic of those we encounter or create as adults? A favored view avers that global communities—religions or regimes—intensify feelings about their aims and other members, and that the beliefs and practices of every constituent system are sanctioned by members' devotion to justice or a God. This is the tradition of gemeinschaft: a fellowship whose participants are sanctified by a worldview, deferential practices, and mutual respect. Gesellschaft favors duties appropriate to roles in systems that calculate alternate ways of satisfying disparate interests or needs. They fill the cultural spaces left vacant when religious or ideological rationales seem mythic or grandiose. Differentiating needs from diversions, duties from opportunities, agents secure themselves with skill, companions, money, or luck: not faith or credulity.

One might have grown up in one of the dominant paradigms of community—a traditional religion or global ideology—where standardized beliefs and practices dominate all aspects of practice and aspiration. But neither type matches the experience of people living in secular cities or states where time and effort are distributed among alliances of different scales and aims. City plasticity is the complement to personal autonomy: finding an interest or need, we learn to satisfy it, often with people whose skills exceed our own. People of all sorts create systems having roles, rules, expectations, rewards, and penalties. This is community as apprenticeship. We remember schools and graduation, but forget that we regularly educate one another, sometimes with gossip but often by explaining what's to be done or by demonstrating how to do it.

Alasdair McIntyre's *After Virtue* is the respectful account of three gemeinschaft communities that sustain pride in their history and traditions by setting themselves apart. They share a strategy: know your virtues and strengths, but also your vulnerabilities. If distance from others is the price for saving communal identity, limit your relations to others and their access to you. Yet distance may be psychological or vocational, not only geographic. Cities are a favored locale because diversity and complexity make sects invisible to people preoccupied by their everyday lives. But this is not a city's principal virtue: each is a natural milieu for training in judgment and choice. Multiple people doing many things test their aims and resolve while going their separate way. One of the oddities ignored is this paradox in urban laissez faire: traditional gemeinschaft communities stabilize by positioning themselves within the flux of their tolerant gesellschaft neighbors.

Communities and their relations provoke many of the tensions that affect social life. Individuals filling their utility's roles worry that their skills and resources aren't adequate to their tasks; they fret that other members aren't equally focused. They're anxious that other systems may interfere with their progress or curtail their opportunities. Holist societies—those of gemeinschaft—reduce these worries because, ideally, individuals, communities, and their relations embody an organizational plan that minimizes conflict for those who satisfy its roles and rules. Meaning—feeling and loyalty—enforce their effects when commitment has a force that is equal or greater than the fear that breaches will be punished. We're gratified that our discipline satisfies a God or the

Good. Gesellschaft societies lack such rationales. Tension pervades them because law and personal discipline are the principal restraints on people and communities encouraged to pursue their interests and opportunities. One isn't sure what other drivers will do or what markets will reward. Gemeinschaft promises to defend us; gesellschaft encourages initiative but magnifies our risk.

Virtual Communities

Technology eases the strain of isolation by helping us find companions known principally or only because they share a passion or an idea. We describe internet assemblies as *virtual*, but that's pejorative when those encounters are no more disreputable than televisits with a physician. There is less passion when reading emails or sharing a Zoom session, but this style of reality-testing seems reliable enough when we use it to pay bills or file taxes. This is efficacy leading feeling, an effect that helps to differentiate these two kinds of affiliation: relations that are emotionally engaging—especially the reciprocities of core or vocational relationships—and those established by the discovery of an attenuated common interest: people known only to one another by way of email or texts. These styles of community have uneven effects: vicarious familiarity is less satisfying than immediacy, yet we want the efficacy that satisfies our interests. Having choice and presence by way of utilities or communities stretching beyond us in electronic space is a bonus. Artists have imaginary spaces; electronic bonding creates surrogate spaces. Oddly socialized while alone, we participate in systems for which we have neither names nor the names of other members. This remakes the fabric of social lives: half in the light of mutual recognition and familiarity; half in the light of a screen. Sitting in the stands with other fans, we share their excitement without knowing their names. A community's electronic members, with only a voice or signature as evidence of their presence, have only half as much grasp.

People don't disperse when going off-line: each was alone before and is still alone. We trade intimacy for access, intensity for mechanical ease. This is the useful complementarity of these two versions of community: their advantages cohere; emotional bonds or utility in the rest of one's life compensates for their absence when paired to electronic abstractions. They needn't compete.

Tension

Social life is simpler, less violent or contentious when order is imposed by a dominant regime: a church, an ideology, or a despot. It doesn't curdle unless one resists the organizing principles or mythology. Societies regulated democratically pay for their laissez-faire principles with disputes that accurately express the contrary interests of their competitors. Law reduces these conflicts when police or courts intervene to prevent violence, but this doesn't avert any next round of disputes. We tolerate this mix of competition and aggression because individuals and their systems are home base for the dynamism we applaud; we value them, but also the contention that makes some dominant while others are submissive or defunct. Let the competition start, but understand Schumpeter's "creative destruction,"[7] and his gloss of blood lust.

Community promises safety, fellowship, and purpose, but communities are sometimes ordinary, deflating, or oppressive. An idealized relationship becomes the anchor we can't shake; or fellowship is genuine, but the community's aims are pernicious and its behavior is malign. What is a member to do when seeking exit or relief from a community still valued for its aims or members? How is one to respond when others are victimized by a community one values?

BELEAGUERED MEMBERS

Waiting too long for service in a café, one is annoyed but free to leave. Costs are greater if one is unhappy at home or work. This may be the effect of disorientation in a new role where anxiety subsides with experience. But it may be evidence that one is unsuited to the role because of temperament or talent. Much of the unhappiness is the effect of systems that are frustrating or punitive after promising comfort or safety. Unhappiness requires patience sufficient to determine its cause. Does a role require skills I don't have, or is the situation intolerable because of partners, management, or its purpose? Is it a job I need, whatever distress I feel? Would my departure disrupt the system severely, or only for the time required to fill my position with an available candidate?

Calculations go back and forth until resolution is decided by an impulsive choice or a change in circumstances: the aggressive colleague leaves, or one is fired. No decision averts frustration because there is a gap between the demands of a role and the psychological profile of anyone appointed to fill it; they may not mesh. Add that a role's demands may change in ways unforeseen when matching tasks to candidates. Gemeinschaft shoehorns people into roles it deems essential, irrespective of their skills or motivation; gesellschaft is messy because agents perpetually calculate how to satisfy roles they barely understand and circumstances they can't foresee. Plato's holistic *Republic* resolved the impasse without asking people what jobs they preferred: it tested and assigned them on the basis of talent and temperament. Their satisfaction was assumed.

Pernicious Communities

Imagine a community congenial to its capable members; they like what it does. But this is Murder, Inc.: safe and comfortable on the inside, it's lethal on the outside. The system's organization and efficiency can't be faulted. Intention is its problem: it lives and moves in the context of enemies: the police, and those of its clients. Malign communities are motivated by jealousy, spite, or profit, though all the criteria for effective communities are in play: self-idealization, loyalty, and purpose. Members are committed, focus is intensified by the exhilaration of power. Is our violence cruel? Not if we justify others' pain as the accident of defending ourselves.

This perspective inverts the attitude expressed by Kant's categorical imperative and Mill's no-harm principle: for them, harm is to be minimized or eliminated when maximizing the good (whatever it may be) is the principal aim. They assumed that harm occurs occasionally but marginally; some agents cause it intentionally, but for the most part it's the effect of thoughtlessness or lack of foresight in complex situations.

That orientation is upended if defense is the priority when the communal fear is damage or extermination. Fear may justify any degree of ferocity in the minds of those feeling it, no matter that they are the aggressors. What are their victims to do? Their situation doesn't call for diplomacy or debate: one fights back with every available weapon or tactic when attacked by those convinced that they must eliminate you to save themselves. This is conflict *in extremis*; we interrupt its trajectory in every way we can, though interventions are not always benign. What does this imply of communal behavior? That its lauded values—fellow feeling, idealization, purpose, and loyalty—may have contrary effects: comfort or security achieved by assaulting others.

Convergence

Boston Red Sox fans, like practicing Catholics or Jews, are a community, but with this difference. Fans are loyal to their team: feelings surge when it wins and sag when it loses, but they typically have no other relation to the team or its other rooters. Community, for them, is an abstraction secured by strong feelings and, perhaps, a hat or badge. Religious communities differ because identity is established by variables that include beliefs, practices, community membership, a rank within the community, and identification with its history or traditions. One may be an anonymous member of a community because loyalty to tribal memory doesn't extend to belief or practice. Others have a stronger claim to membership: they believe and practice with others as their faith prescribes.

These variations trade intensity and immersion for autonomy and distance. They illustrate the error of supposing that fans need attend every home game or that coreligionists satisfy all the variables for religious identity mentioned above. Communities are often more diffuse than tradition demands: some members are core; others are privately loyal but behaviorally remote. What does variability imply about connection? That passion and belief are sufficient for personal commitment, but not for engagement. We needn't discount fans who never attend games or believers who never join a congregation, though commitments that never rise to the demands of participation and reciprocity don't stabilize their communities. Sustaining members make their reliability known to others by satisfying the markers of tribal identity: strong feelings; belief in community values and aims; meaning (discussed below); actions that exhibit those values; collaboration with their community's other members; and loyalty to it and them. Satisfying all six variables is evidence that people internalize community membership as an essential expression of personal identity. It distinguishes them from people whose loyalties are firm, though inclinations or circumstances reduce them to peripheral expressions of communal identity. Are they a community's members, or merely its satellites?

The criteria for community membership are also questionable because those described above—especially communities-of-interest and -meaning—are too rigid for popular variations. It is communities-at-large that are pertinent to the tides sweeping through a society's politics, tastes, or sport. All would regard fashion updates as ephemeral, though people enjoy the fellowship they excite. No matter that the provocation is an idea, film, or style: we respond because the mood pleases us, and because enjoying ourselves with others is social comfort: why resist a feeling that's widely shared? Communities of taste may seem to lack direction, like flocks of starlings wheeling and diving unpredictably. Yet participants rarely seem confused about a style's variations; they may not know where it's going, but they quickly learn where it's gone.

How do we explain a fashion's sure-footed progress, never having to explain itself while advancing in ways that resemble a random walk? It can't be explained when proof that a preference is worthy is just the fact that it's chosen. We sometimes look back critically when taste has an altered focus, but we're usually unembarrassed by all but its most lurid mistakes. Why this passion for styles and agendas fixed by other people? Because this is community of a different sort, community in which collaboration is imitation: one participates by wearing or voicing its emblems. Nietzsche's *Genealogy of Morals* describes artistic genius as an ability to exceed conventional limits by considering what others were too rigid or timorous to imagine.[8] But most of us are not artists; we acquire our tastes and habits by osmosis, from others.

Community is learned in two ways, one local and specific, the other more diffuse. Families, businesses, and governance are local:

members assemble for a task or because of sentiment. The other form is a cultural tide; it floods regions of the whole. Communities of the first sort have more or less explicit and specific meanings, idealizations, and purposes; members have roles and tasks. The tide is different: people are passive when receiving a taste or style, though active when showing it to their neighbors. This isn't community in the modes described previously because it has neither purpose nor the collaborations required to achieve it. Yet the mechanisms explaining its efficiency—fear of being different, imitation, and comfort—are plain. Their effects may be most apparent to observers from cultures with different sensibilities; they may see the tide without understanding why it moves or where it's going.

Which of the styles cited above do these communities exhibit? They fit no rubric precisely because they're amorphous: passing interests mix with gossipy chatter. They remind us that communities vary across a range: from stable and tight to giddy and loose.

Chapter Two

Infrastructure

The previous chapter describes communities' apparent features. This chapter describes their context and mechanics.

Comparison

The solidarity emphasized by gemeinschaft is focused by a religion or ideology. Its members see needs and aims from the perspective of a conceptual framework, a narrative that describes God's creation or conditions for realizing the Good. All should defer to its teachings or to the prophetic voices honored for transmitting them. Duties to be satisfied are a complement to the punishments feared if one ignores the practices commanded. Gemeinschaft is focused by its virtuous paradigms: the good mother, noble leader, exemplary priest. These are gemeinschaft's moral examples: it would have us be godly or good. Productivity and collaboration are less important than exemplifying its perfected forms. Gemeinschaft is, in this respect, as much aesthetic as moral: children should learn, adults will exhibit the conduct it prescribes.

Gesellschaft is an assembly of utilities regulated by laws of contract and rights-of-way. It construes society as a complex of people and systems satisfying personal needs in circumstances that are principally local. Wanting productivity, it emphasizes the collaborations of people who are transactional and utilitarian. Because one solution doesn't fit all concerns and because challenges are often complex, it emphasizes initiative, tolerance, and interdependence. Needing solutions for local problems, it expects disruptions.

Gesellschaft dispenses with totalizing narratives; it denigrates gemeinschaft's virtues as the fluff of sentiment. Regarding fellowship as a useful social lubricant, it has no essential regard for community, apart from its dedication to the free choice of partners and tasks. Participants may regret the loss of moral empathy, purpose, or a consensual view of reality; but many of them enjoy freedom and prosperity. We lived—or imagined living—within a whole that was coherent and good because created and regulated by a power infinitely greater than ourselves. Now, when that persuasion seems more mythic than likely, we achieve equanimity by relying on ourselves and whatever collaborations we can arrange.

Basic needs are universal, yet gesellschaft responds more effectively than gemeinschaft because it isn't burdened by having to satisfy them within the terms of formulae incidental to the problems at hand. This was Tönnies's prediction for us. If we agree that extreme views—Hobbes's or Hume's—are clarifying, then this is too.

> In the Gesellschaft, as contrasted with the *Gemeinschaft*, we find no action that can be derived from an a priori and necessarily existing unity; no actions, therefore, which manifest the will and the spirit of the unity even if performed by the individual; no actions which, in so far as they are performed by the individual, take place on behalf of those united with him. In the Gesellschaft such actions do not exist. On the contrary, here everybody is by himself and isolated, there exists a condition of tension against all others. Their sphere of activity and power are sharply separated, so that everybody refuses to everyone else contact with and admittance to his sphere: i.e., intrusions are regarded as hostile acts.[1]

We aren't this crude; our individualism isn't as extreme as Hobbes or Tönnies imagined it could be. But if there is a continuum from the

INFRASTRUCTURE 35

extremes of gemeinschaft to those of gesellschaft, this passage expresses a recognizable limit.

Gemeinschaft makes its version of interiority plain by demanding obeisance. "Thou shalt have no other God before me": let your commitment be plain; do as you're commanded. Doing it creates affinities—the sameness of the devout—not the distinct roles of people having complementary tasks. Gesellschaft is a paradox: it is efficient but often incapable of appeasing the agents who do its work. They go from task to task, rewarded for work they do, though never relieved of having to do more. Yet many have the benefits of family, vocation, or neighborhood, hence the means for transforming instrumental relations into something closer to friendship and well-being.

Disciplinary Social Spaces

These are spaces of three kinds: public or private spaces (city streets or schools) where behavior satisfies rules or roles; physical spaces where actions are circumscribed by geometry (playing fields) or social practice (traffic laws); or prescriptive conceptual spaces (societies they regulate).

Soccer and American football are played on fields that are featureless but for borders and line markings. Baseball diamonds exhibit the specificities of their game: a pitcher's mound and batter's box; first, second, and third base; an outfield. Societies are prefigured in an analogous way by their communities-of-accord: each is a context—a site—for communities positioned within it. But playing fields are plots of land; these are conceptual designs prescribing the character of pertinent social behaviors and relations. They clarify or prescribe the generic character of social relations and their effects (marriage or traffic laws but sometimes no specific version of either). They align, for their acculturated residents, with the effects of habit and conscience or inclination; each prefigures what we would or wouldn't, should or shouldn't do. This is the power of gemeinschaft and gesellschaft: each is a coherent abstraction, an idealization, and a backdrop for the more specific details of societies we have or wish to create. Yet each is irreconcilable with the other: they oppose an authoritarian hierarchical society where personal identities are fixed by one's roles to one that is open, flat, and pluralistic, a society where social identity is the function of available opportunities and the choices made within a web of (mostly) neutral rules. Each model dominates the terrains of its application when variations usually resolve to one, the other, or a mélange of the two. Each is higher order in the respect that its variations may themselves be generic: there are Confucian as well as Catholic versions of gemeinschaft. Virtue varies with their differences: it requires discipline in China; piety in Rome. gesellschaft is also variable: Texas or New York, Britain or America. Are there societies or cultures that exhibit the features of both? The France of Rousseau's *Social Contract* is an example: pragmatic *liberté* and totalizing *fraternité*—autonomy and solidarity.

Each community-of-accord is a style embedded in the self-perceptions, expectations, and responses of people who are mutually recognizable because educated in the duties and expectations it prefigures; they're tolerant of their neighbors' values, and responsive to their aims. Yet disciplinary spaces materialize over time, sometimes inconsistently. Both attitudes—gemeinschaft and gesellschaft—are consolidated in cultures where each seems as unalterable as the local street plan. But how deep do their effects go; are they merely stylistic conventions, forms that might be stripped away exposing an underlying social policy? No, these are alternate determinations—qualifications—of a society's elemental, determinable form. It can be made determinate in either way but can't be experienced prior to having one of these determinate forms or one of the mixed forms that merge the two.

Ideology, power, and experience have pushed societies one way or the other. Both may be stable for a time, because each has a rationale favored by some. Living in a society of one sort, we may know enough of the other to admire its strengths. Yet their parity is disputed because we oppose the side we prefer to a discredited version of the other. Consider their differences when using moderate examples of each: gemeinschaft as coherent stability with social care; gesellschaft as opportunity, initiative, and tolerant diversity. How could we justify choosing between them? Writers can usually be relied on to explain why a design is preferred, by speculating about its mythological origins or sponsor, but imagination is less compelling than deeply held values and traditions of social practice.

Politics, whether dominated by power or ideas, often turns about contested plans for qualifying one design with features from the other: social care from gemeinschaft; initiative from gesellschaft; Mill's *Utilitarianism* versus his *On Liberty*. Considering the two at once, we realize how protean our societies are, as though they perpetually seek, but can't sustain, a steady state of one sort before reverting to the other. Are there alternate templates for communities-of-accord—a third, fourth, or more? Imagination is often reduced to these two because of their contrariety: societies that are open or closed, pious or freethinking. Community leavens the conflict by incorporating the holism of families, businesses, and friendships within a society whose diversity proves its tolerance.

Why is this accommodation possible? Because health, education, and safety are common needs sometimes satisfied by global solutions, and because of the higher-order community-of-accord binding the residents of every stable society, whether it be one of gemeinschaft or gesellschaft. Each requires that residents accede to the form and laws of the commonwealth established by people who assent to the duties of their disciplinary space. Kant supposed that assent is formal: we're to affirm the rational principle—his categorical imperative—whose applications avert damage to our shared space. Rousseau's emphasis on *fraternité* makes a similar claim while making its duties interpersonal, historical, and local.

Could one be resident in a disciplinary space while deploring its form and rules? Charles Taylor's objection to gesellschaft's atomizing effects is made in that spirit: he objects that the individualism of Western political economies is antithetical to the spiritual accord fostered by his church. The civil bargain required of his neighbors—to live and let live—dismays him. People grateful for the Enlightenment can only shrug; yet gesellschaft is vulnerable, because the diversity it tolerates includes people and communities that oppose the loose community-of-accord regulating its social forms and relations. Does this difference of opinion affect the communities formed in gesellschaft societies? We have only to compare an orthodox religious service to a Quaker meeting to know that it does: one survives the decline of gemeinschaft societies in

38 COMMUNITY

the West while regretting the demise of doctrinal authority and moral clarity; the other welcomes tolerance, diversity, and choice.

Structure

The next four sections discuss some principal aspects of community structure.

SYSTEMS

Static systems satisfy procedures that make no difference to the character of the items they organize: things filed alphabetically, the notes of a score. Communities are dynamic systems created when causal reciprocities bind their members. Their relations create complex stable systems whose individual members are their prime parts: the spouses in a marriage, a team's players.

An airline's passengers buy tickets before being taken where they want to go. Community enriches instrumental relationships with fellowship, an addition that stabilizes systems by intensifying the loyalty of their members. Increments that come with feeling or interpretation may seem trivial in relationships that are otherwise mechanical and reliable: we wonder if penguins warming their eggs during a blizzard require feeling to do it. Yet knowing of people who seem indifferent to others, we credit caregivers for feelings vital to community well-being. Nurses and teachers are notable for their intermediate role: the care they show professionally mirrors what others do on more intimate terms. Does this blur the distinction between meaning and utility; or is it an expression of shadow-communities, intimations that the reciprocities binding people in various roles can transform utilities into something closer to communities-of-meaning?

RELATIONS

Aristotle supposed that substance is the primary ontological category, and that living things are freestanding while having natures determining

INFRASTRUCTURE   39

their development from birth to death. Development was said to be
governed by four causes: material, efficient, formal, and final. Human
bodies are material; DNA and our learned culture are the forms determining the effects of personal evolution; metabolism and conversation
are efficient causes, all acting within constraints imposed by formal
causes. Final cause is that-for-the-sake-of-which we act. Some aims
are trivial or ephemeral; others are the ends for which we organize.

Aristotle distinguished relations constitutive of a living thing's
development (from seed or zygote to death) and those occurring, because
of relations incidental to its natural evolution: things glued together, for
example. The latter are accidents; the former are essential to life. Are
communities rightly construed on analogy to living systems, because,
if so, relations binding their members—human bonding—are natural
rather than accidental. But do communities have form: intrinsic natures
achieved as they evolve? Form in living bodies, some machines, and
many natural events (hurricanes and volcanoes) gives them a degree
of self-sufficiency: their actions are initiated by factors within them,
not always or only because of interactions with other things. Relative
self-sufficiency explains the impression that communities, too, are
monadic: causal reciprocity integrates their members while insulating
them from disruptions to a degree required by their tasks, enabled by
their resources.

Appealing to Aristotle's ideas of cause and substance seems antique.
Why do it? Because his ideas are clarifying when carefully applied.
Hume resisted Aristotle, grounding his claim that sensory data are the
only referents for cause and effect by arguing that what we construe
as material existence is the force and vivacity of our impressions:[2]
causation, he said, is their constant conjunction. But Hume's argument
is belied by everyday experience: the dentist who cures my pain has no
direct access to my impressions, though he fixes the tooth causing it. I
suppose that percepts are natural signs representing causes and effects
in the extramental world. Acknowledging common sensibles—people,
teeth, and things of many sorts—invites this other account of cause
and effect: causation is energy exchange or its inhibition.

Processes causing the breath and blood flow that enable perception
are examples. Descartes exploited this information in his physiological

drawings; Hume ignored it because he denied that we have a capacity for inferring from impressions to their extra-mental conditions, though he acknowledged that practical life warrants inferences contrary to the implications of his skeptical arguments.[3] The difference of percepts and things perceived might have been plainer to Hume had his sight been altered by cataract surgery: cloudy vision transformed within hours by the clarity and vivid colors experienced when eyes scan the ambient world through plastic lenses. Which of these appearances best represents the actual world? Ask a spectroscope.

Community requires a willingness to engage one's fellows in actions responsive to an interest or need. This, too, is causal reciprocity, though its character seems disguised if one's example is crafted to the requirements of third-party observers: they see you throw the ball before I hit it back to you. The behavior vital to communities is observable—people playing, working, or praying together—but the principal work of reciprocity is disguised because it's intrapsychic: seeing me do what you anticipated confirms your expectation and provokes your response. Stable repetitions of the actions passing between us are inexplicably coherent if one ignores the calibrated subjective processes that provoke and explain them. This is our mutual attunement. Its conditions are intrapsychic, though their result is the reliable exchange of expectations and confirming actions.

Causal reciprocity is responsible for the mechanical systems basic to the creation and stability of communities. They are established when members bond; they stabilize when agents act in ways that enable satisfaction of their complementary roles: students and teachers, or a team's players as they adjust to one another. Positive feedback is energizing: participants are provoked to greater effort or initiative by partners or their corporate success: the orchestra plays better, the team wins. Negative feedback is the control that enables stability: drivers stop taking risks that threaten their safety; we turn down the volume of a radio that's too loud. Stability and coherence are not, however, sufficient measures of efficacy: teams may be steady but mediocre. More than reciprocity, the quality of play is a measure of talent and organization.[4]

The causal reciprocities responsible for establishing communities were already effective when they created the utilities from which communities emerge. The difference between communities-of-interest and communities-of-meaning lies in the identity of their causes. In utilities, causes are the tasks, skills, organization, resources, and motivations of the partners; in the other, causes are members' shared meanings, including interpretations or idealizing emotions, loyalties, and intentions. Bonding under duress explains the creation of work teams, but not communities-of-meaning. Their generation requires the subtle byplay of people made secure when emotions or beliefs provoking closer relations to others are correctly read and reciprocated. Though sometimes, fellowship and community emerge in the teams—as with firemen and platoons—organized for a task.

Fellow feeling, loyalty, trust, and habit are community enablers; they stabilize because their motivators, need and interest, persist when satisfied. Yet subjectivity is ontologically suspect when mind is identified with neural or hormonal activity. Believing that everything mental has physical conditions only, we're quick to make the strange inference that any mental event not already explained in physiological terms is a nonevent postulated by the clumsy but congenial folk psychology that speaks of hunger, anger, and affection. Do we acknowledge that people love and grieve? Because, if so, we distinguish phenomena that are well known from explanations that aren't yet adequate to their complexity.

We acknowledge that the bonding achieved by causal reciprocities is often infused with feeling and significance, that friendship becomes something deeper when Jack and Jill marry. Few would argue that the intensities motivating them are trivial, fewer still would likely tell them that they don't have these feelings or that they're epiphenomenal. Subjectivity is the array of processes occurring within an organic system able to read and control some of its internal states. Why call it epiphenomenal, so acausal, because much of the processes responsible for these powers are still unknown? Why should a simple surmise—it's all neural, hormonal, or muscular—explain complex states of feeling and control that more detailed hypotheses may someday explain?

ORGANIZATIONS AND ASSOCIATIONS

Utilities are typically organizations designed for aims they satisfy by filling essential roles with skilled agents. Their principal motive is efficiency, not fellowship. Communities sometimes emerge from smaller utilities when mutually respectful partners become friends; though, conversely, families become organizations when working parents rationalize costs and routines. Associations, too, are communities joined by an interest, though members aren't differentiated by their roles; each is a friend, fan, or fellow believer. They generate emotional energy as people show their beliefs and feelings, thereby mirroring, confirming, and provoking those of other members: I believe because of seeing that you believe.

The unity of organizations is the effect of designs that integrate their roles in service to their aims. Associations seem fragile by comparison because they lack the integration entailed by internal organization and a functional boundary, and because the excitement binding members often depends on external events and conditions: fans who celebrate when their team wins a game. Friendships and fan clubs are associations, schools are organizations; some communities are both. Quakers have little or no organization; the Catholic Church is both tightly organized and a fellowship whose participants mirror the beliefs and practices of other members. Political parties suffer the vulnerability of having just one strength: however well organized, they usually fail to sustain the passions of effectively organized religions. Catholic history is evidence that communities having both forms are more viable than those having one or the other.

Associations resemble organizations in the respect that both are affected by the two kinds of feedback. Organizations are switched on or off by role-players who goad one another to accomplish an aim; or they correct and control one another if the process goes awry. Their activators in associations are principally feelings or interpretations frustrated or satisfied by events the agents don't control. Think of a couple newly acquainted or a team newly assembled: these are people responding to one another for a first time, each wanting coherence but easily confounded when testing the other's responses.

ETHOS AND AFFINITIES

Societies, families, neighborhoods, or vocations are tight enough to be identifiable: one knows who does or doesn't qualify for membership.

But some associations are diffuse: who likes hip-hop, who knows what's in or out? This is information and feeling exuded rather than streamed. We understand information disseminated by books, essays, or news reports, but affinities of this intensity aren't well understood, though their decentered force and authority are recognizable. Their content and connections seem indeterminate: one isn't sure what's there, its origin, or how it crystallized. Media correspondents strain to keep up; but ask knowledgeable people: can they identify their community's other members, trends, and tendencies? They may hesitate briefly, but they do know or think they do.

Imagine a congenial restaurant: people at nearby tables don't know one another, but each hears and feels a tide of well-being to which all respond. This is positive feedback, a response that also spreads when all are morose. Cities express this ambiguity when an iconic team wins or loses a critical game; it dominates feelings whether the local economy is good or bad. This is the communal agitation of people responding to circumstances and one another. Is there synchrony between pockets of local froth and society at large; can local attitudes and feelings galvanize the whole? That may happen if material conditions—governance or the economy—promotes a surge in one direction or the other.

Ethos is a style of association for which we have few words, though settlements—cities and towns, especially—are often distinguished by it. Consider any two that are familiar, then notice that each has a distinctive energy—a quality more than motion and noise, expressed wherever people gather. Cities that look alike don't feel the same. Consider, too, that the behavior galvanizing ethos doesn't require an aim or design. People enjoy bars, dance and concert halls because of the emotional energies they arouse; one doesn't have to know people at nearby seats or tables to experience their enthusiasm. Moving within a room or hall, it spreads osmotically. Those affected are described as participants or customers, not as members; they establish their community's emotional energy field by making themselves vulnerable to one another. People unmoved are silent; no one breaks the spell.

Tides of purpose or feeling sometimes vitalize communities as they assemble; social froth becomes a self-conscious demand for conditions—material or legislative—that defend the security of all by stabilizing coherence. Affiliating communities may impel the formation of networks or alliances that express a coherent general will. Yet the spontaneity of their formation is unreliable because unforeseeable. We prefer predictable regimes imposed by rituals or rules that offer safety and meaning to people unnerved when loyalties and duties are a jumble. Communities of a different sort are a contrast to these enthusiasms. They are established in two steps: first, by a personal interest; second, by using *community* to name the common interest: bird-watcher, trainspotter, poet. Like an association's members, those sharing these passions may have no organization; unlike them, they lack the interactions essential to fellowship. The internet somewhat compensates for their anonymity because it makes them discoverable, though affinity long antedates current technology: readers had their books, collectors their stamps. Think of people sitting together in a concert hall, listening to music while alone. These are communities-of-interest, though, unlike utilities, participants may never engage like-minded others.

Variables

Utilities are efficient: what's the task; are there available personnel and resources; what's to be done? Yet all seems mysterious if it's communities-of-meaning that invite access. Their spontaneity is anomalous with the means-ends planning that distinguishes communities-of-interest; one can't prepare for the spontaneity of emotional bonding or shared understanding. It's said that pearls form in response to the irritation caused by a grain of sand: communities-of-meaning are their analogue. People usually separate when an aim is satisfied; yet sometimes, when each evokes positive feelings in another, they form a relationship that survives the reason for their meeting.

This is a beginning more sentimental than stories of musicians who adore their work and colleagues after bitter memories of years spent practicing their instruments. It doesn't describe children inducted into a religious community while attending its schools and learning its rituals. This is, perhaps, a reason for ambivalence when thinking of community: is it liberating or controlling, a relationship that opens us to others or one that others impose? These are some variables.

COMMUNAL STYLES

These are six community styles, each with its distinctive orientation: (1) communities are core (families and friendships); (2) vocational or commercial (schools or businesses); (3) holistic (religions or states); (4) professional (physicians and their patients); (5) competitive (athletic leagues or bridge clubs); or (6) casual (cordial neighbors). These are alliances distinguished by their aims, duties, and the feelings or expectations of their members. Each requires that members discern its character and duties, and that they have skills appropriate to its tasks. Community's emotional palette—intimate or remote—is variable, with differences correlated to generic, functional differences. Each style promotes a standard of reliability appropriate to its aim and the self-interest of its participants. Vocational relationships are typically more remote than those of family, though warmer than commercial or professional bonds (to stores or doctors); there's a limit to one's anguish for a losing team. Participating in communities of each kind, one is rarely surprised that duties and expectations vary from one to another.

Communities-of-accord—gemeinschaft and gesellschaft—are also utilities sometimes having meaning, with the difference that formation of the six is provoked by circumstances of specific kinds. Those of accord are the disciplinary spaces—the background communities—in which the others form.

LOCALITY

Community evokes neighborly feelings, cooperation, and purpose. Propinquity was once thought to be essential to community, but no more; we vaunt technologies that enable remote surgeries and Zoom meetings. People need fellowship as much as ever, yet current social organization often requires efficiency more than good feeling. The implications for community are severe because it doesn't emerge from workers indifferent to the anonymity of their partners. No idealizing stories fill the voids with emotional significance when feeling needs proximity; it doesn't register as well when communicated electronically.

Each scale of community—core, corporate, or holistic—comprises several or many social systems, some that evoke feeling and loyalty, but many appreciated only for their utility: schools are the way to a better job; learning is otherwise incidental. This bloodless quality—too many systems reduced to utilitarian values—makes people despair: we sentimentalize the idea of village life or a piety we never knew. There are people who still feel these intensities, but they are, for many, sentiments known from books or films. The community lives of McIntyre's *After Virtue*—each emphatically local—don't arouse us because we value autonomy and its enabling education more than theological imagination or tribal loyalty. Yet we're troubled by losing the shared purpose that religion or ideology supplied. Rousseau thought that secular holidays would provoke *fraternité*; Dewey believed that shared reverence for a constitution and laws would make friends of fellow citizens however near or far. Believing, with Mill's *On Liberty*, that reasons are compelling, he discounted emotion and immediacy as goads to community. Yet fellowship comes more easily if experience and opportunities are roughly similar for people who talk, face to face, about needs and interests.

Where could we go to immerse ourselves in a grander cause if local encounters were insufficient? There might be salvation in a global ideology, though principal ideas of gemeinschaft failed because their rallying points were destructive (wars), more fantasy than substance (theologies), or because their abstractions (ideal societies) were more portentous than feasible. What are we to do if the idea of community is still compelling? Is it sufficient that we rethink the possibilities of locality: would I know more of the conditions for public order if I knew the intentions of fellow drivers or pedestrians; or is it enough that people defer to the same traffic laws? Law and the comfort of knowing that strangers respect it are the conditions for personal freedom and the safest conditions for enjoying it within utilitarian systems whose members are mostly strangers. This is the paradox of instrumental systems drained of fellowship, though ever more efficient.

Community Formation and Membership

We clarify community formation and membership by examining alternate versions of community: a church's active members, then teams, and families.

INFRASTRUCTURE 47

Suppose affection and mutual care are mediated by religious services and a narrative expressing the beliefs to which members defer. The second dominates the first because congregants who dissent from church doctrine lose the esteem of their fellows. It isn't enough that skeptics enjoy a society's songs and rituals or the company of other participants: pretending to exalt its inspiring ideas while privately scorning them is perceived as hypocrisy. A sturdy core defends its beliefs and traditions. Yet religious communities are fragile wherever science, education, and a secular wind have reduced religious conviction to the perimeters of local neighborhoods. Sects that were once mutually suspicious now affiliate, sometimes sharing their quarters. Why this mutual tolerance? Because believers living where religion is incidental to autonomy and economy have much in common. They share a posture that is essentially defensive: you're welcome to your beliefs if I can have mine.

McIntyre's *After Virtue* implies that a community's integrity is diminished by an evolution that reduces its autonomy, because communities turn porous and feeble when members defer to economic and social interests vital to everyone's well-being. This, too, is community of a sort, community-at-large; we share the expectation that instrumentality is an enabling power when the gemeinschaft of religion or ideology is displaced by gesellschaft and its utilitarian diversity. Or, if we're lucky, the fabric of family, friendship, work, and neighborhood is stitched together experientially in ways that create a fabric sturdy enough to replace its theological or ideological ancestors.

Teams are the apotheosis of locality and a counter to the alleged universality of religion or ideology. Cities and towns come together in spasms of hope or anxiety as their teams compete for championships or merely as they play a rival. The collaborations of team members require purpose and complementary skills, relationships of agency and accord, not always mutual affection. Families and friendships bend the other way: feeling and reciprocity—mutual loyalty and sentiment—are their sustaining condition. Friendship begins in mutual recognition; families evolve from this inception. Their children resemble people who join a long-established church. Family stories, rituals, and priorities are learned; family histories are their context. A religion's formalities survive for centuries; its communities perpetuate them with as little

48 COMMUNITY

deviation as possible. Families are different because each diverges from its predecessors; it may repeat their values but not their contingencies or the psychological accommodations each makes to its circumstances.

One principal virtue is common to communities of all three kinds, religions, teams, and families; each functions as a unit: an association in the case of religions, an organization in that of teams, something of both in families. Each is an expression of the enabling social glue that relieves the burdens of autonomy. Having partners, we aren't required to learn or do everything on our own, without the advice of someone better informed. This is sociality: each person as guide and support for several or many others.

VALUE

Communities aren't formed or sustained unless valued. Those who favor them are sometimes observers (grandparents, perhaps), but more often, they're members who value the community for itself, other members, or its aims. Communities that lose sight of their values often survive as clubs or tribes, though now they're contentious, aggressive, and mean. Members remain out of habit or they prize their community's utility (its effects or the contacts one makes). This is an issue for gesellschaft because loyalty to communities that emerge from utilities may be shallow if profit is the principal binder. Fearing this outcome is one motive for romanticizing uniformity in religious or ideological devotions; their associations seem invulnerable when members bond. The holism they embody makes gemeinschaft seem timeless.

FOREGROUND AND BACKGROUND

Every community is foreground to an enabling or permissive background, a community-of-accord. Rather than a material resource or focus, it combines permission with proscription: communal practices that would be anathema in a totalizing religion may be enabled by a society that's open to personal choice and experiment.

How is a background chosen? How is the choice justified? Disciplinary spaces are more often endorsed than chosen: we affirm the one in which we live if it's congenial to our beliefs and values. The gemeinschaft of religions and ideologies is dominated by narratives that justify values by fixing beliefs. But which of the two constrains the other: does belief control value or the reverse? Ideologies start with ideas of the good—freedom or justice, for example—before constructing a narrative that vindicates its values. Religion goes the other way when it describes a reality in which a god commands its values. Zealots of both inspirations are almost unique for wanting to deny space to competitors. They're frustrated by the fluid, often equivocal transition from gemeinschaft to gesellschaft, from space perceived as a controlled plenum to the open space where difference is acknowledged and tolerated. Any version of an activity—tennis or ping-pong—can assert its right to dominate all the space in which it's a presence, but it's likely to be apologetic when making its claim in societies that enjoy flourishing alternatives. Skiing fanatics don't mind ice skating, Chinese restaurants compete peaceably with American diners. Gesellschaft is preferred by those who share this tolerance. Its partisans explain themselves by saying that contested issues—the best constitution—don't have definitive answers; or they distance themselves from disputes about a god's preferred religion. This conclusion provokes a different question: what sort of education would be required to convince competing sides that there is good evidence and plausible reasons for many hypotheses but no definitive evidence for any? Gesellschaft isn't perturbed by residual ambiguities. Space is ample; there is room for fantasies of all sorts; let them compete. What we don't want are their nervous confrontations. They occur when having a dedicated region of social space isn't sufficient to a system claiming authority over others, or when others aren't entitled to any space because a domineering community claims that it embodies the true religion or affords the only plausible regime.

Conviction falters when the narratives affirming a gemeinschaft's beliefs or values are challenged by the demand for justifying reasons or evidence. This is contentious: how do we back up to defend Enlightenment objections to authoritarian religions or regimes? Is it enough to point out, in the spirit of Plato's *Euthyphro*, that no evidence or argument proves the existence of a god? Do we retreat to Plato's *Republic* to argue the worth of a holist good or to Aristotle's *Politics* for the benefits of a society dominated by its productive middle class? We don't do the first out of respect for religious sensibilities, or the second because the Enlightenment argument is compelling: there is no justification, coercion apart, for capitulating to someone else's credulity.

Change

Community is mourned for the loss of its global condition: is there no enveloping system of beliefs and practices in which family members, believers, workers, and friends are joined; no idea, no church that makes us resonate as one? The conditions for participation have altered. Before, they required loyalty, piety, affect, and mutual recognition by a community's other members. More recently—the past two or three centuries—personal identity is fixed by one's roles: I am what I do, not so much by my place in a community where others believe, hope, or feel as I do. Mutual expectations and recognition are practical and cerebral rather than emotional. Before we were cosseted, defended, and reassured; now, amid complexity that exceeds anyone's grasp, we choose our loyalties. Autonomy is a point of pride; anomie is a cost we bear. Partners are collaborators; we expect them to perform as their tasks require. Why they do it is incidental when cooperation makes this simpler demand: that each understand his or her role while able to fill it. Efficacy is our principal value: pitcher and catcher secure their reciprocity when each knows how to throw and catch a ball. They're likely to know one another's names, but that's unnecessary when working together is their only task.

Notice a schismatic fracture in this response: we're distanced from partners because we've become their appraisers. We're judged by the very people to whom we're coupled in family, friendship, or work. Tradition, shared feelings, and values are incidental when efficacy and its effects dominate understanding of what we do and how we do it. Several factors created this change: economy's practical effects are apparent because we're consequentialists—show us what you do, and how well you do it—and because we're familiar with money, work, and opportunity. We idealize competition when it provokes initiative and imagination, though its effects are alienating if community fractures when winners thrive without regard for those who fail. We discount them because sympathy is shallow if winners keep their rewards whatever the cost to losers.

These practical effects somewhat disguise their theological and philosophic antecedents. The Platonism in Descartes's *Meditations* is an example. It invokes innate ideas (like Plato's Forms) that enable the cooperative deliberations of minds that are otherwise mutually indifferent: we think independently, while capable of thinking the same things. Add that Descartes's *cogito* avers that intuitive thinkers, like the liberated prisoner in Plato's cave, are psychologically and ontologically autonomous: they seek clear and distinct ideas irrespective of conceptual confusions or ambiguous relations to other thinkers. For what is there to learn of myself from others if nothing is better known to mind than mind itself?[5]

Luther diminished the role of empathy or cooperation in moral practice when he argued that moral sense is present in each person because implanted there by the God who creates individual souls[6]: morality, this implies, directs behavior and dictates one's judgments of others irrespective of our relations to them. Kant's emphasis on moral law assembles sovereign agents by establishing a universal, because logical, basis for moral assent, one requiring no relations—no communication—among them. These are thinkers who encouraged community's dissolution by provoking the skepticism that reduced religious stories to sentiment and mythology. Their disruptive effects were described by Tönnies and Simmel: Tönnies when he distinguished gemeinschaft and gesellschaft; Simmel when he described "metropolitan man," a *flaneur* who enjoys cosmopolitan tastes without having to do more than move about among the misfits and characters who make his city interesting.[7]

Communities such as those described in MacIntyre's *After Virtue* are bound by attitudes and behaviors sanctioned by centuries of tradition. Each member lives within the weave of practices that require no justification; there are generational changes, but evolution is slow. It doesn't accelerate until freedom and efficiency displace sentiment and coherence. Jane Jacobs's *The Death and Life of Great American Cities* describes the risks to a city neighborhood as rationalization reshapes its neighbors and streets. Small stores disappear, residents leave or move as buildings with elevators and modern plumbing replace tenements. This is gesellschaft, neighborhoods reformed for the reasonable aim of living better.[8]

Affect matters less if one doesn't hear or know one's neighbors. Does it reemerge in relations centered by material advantages? Could it be evoked by recognition that complementary tasks generate an effect approved by partners who are otherwise distracted? Orchestral musicians, like all team members, feel pride when playing well together. But what if the scale of collaboration exceeds a partner's ability to believe that he or she is responsible to any degree for its success because none can discern personal effects in the large-scale projects employing them? Do workers care if the corporate result is good or bad, or whether it's achieved? Neither may matter if people are well paid, whatever they do.

Gesellschaft isn't designed to sabotage community; that's an unintended effect of rationalizing the traditional systems—of church, work, neighborhoods, schools, and homes—in which people bond. Members of a society reformed by technology or efficient organization may come to feel gratitude for their collaborators, though the feeling is incidental to their society's rationale. Dewey recognized this effect in the two late chapters of his *The Public and Its Problems* mentioned above. One describes a society organized by rules and laws making it coherent and effective; the other—called "The Great Community"—emphasizes the emotional bonds of members proud of their society and respectful of those with whom they've created it. But this is a very refined affection, one too dilute for any occasion less focused than the Fourth or fourteenth of July.

One imagines regimes that promote tribal authority with stories of fellowship and unity, though success is thwarted by a complex of unrelated causes. Capitalist economies encourage competition and the durable inequalities they provoke. We might try to disguise their effects with a story that postulates a unifying power and its good intentions—a god or corporation—but this was gemeinschaft's discredited cure for injustice and bad outcomes. A different cause is our confusion and ambivalence about freedom. For we rarely clarify our understanding of the complementary freedoms: *freedom from* and *freedom to.* Exemption from the autocratic demands of church and state was a principal demand of Enlightenment thought and parliamentary democracy. But knowing what we don't like or want was and is straightforward; learning basic skills—what to choose, how to find partners—is harder. Wealth seems the better destiny because it requires fewer choices and less energy; it's also preferable because of forgiving reckless choices. But freedom to choose and act is a discipline: why learn to play the cello if you can play a recording of others playing it better? Wanting or demanding freedom from people or institutions that tell us what to believe or do, more often poor than rich, we shun hard choices and the partnerships they require. This is an irony of our time: *freedom to* is demanding; technology saves us from having to exercise it: music is streamed; planes fly themselves. Communities may once have formed about utilitarian systems that provided those effects, but they don't form where those systems aren't needed. Having freedom, we avert having to use it; comfortable in our passivity, we're content if reality is addressed by machines that manage it for us. Will there be any urgency to the actual world when films and games make it all but indistinguishable from fantasy?

Last Thoughts

Community infrastructure has a determinable form that tolerates diversity. Difference within limits isn't a surprise, given our many aims and the ways of achieving them. Yet gesellschaft favors prudence; isn't feeling an irrational force, one that impedes effective choice? That is often true, though no barrier to the reality that feeling is often low-level cognition, one telling us whom to trust and when to trust them, information critical to collaboration or conflict, to utility and community.

Chapter Three

Meaning and Normativity

People having similar tastes or interests are sometimes described as communities, though their members may share an affinity but no contact. The residents of towns ruled by an autocrat's strictures may defer to a regime's practices while remaining indifferent to its beliefs and to one another; they participate in its community by virtue of living in places it dominates. We need better illustrations of community, examples signifying the cognitive and emotional responses that enable communal relations. They begin in shared understandings or emotional exchanges; they evolve as people pursue an aim to which they're committed or an interest they share.

The principal sections below are "Meaning," and "Normativity." Each is followed by its more specific expressions.

Meaning

Meaning is significance, as in the phrase, This is meaningful. Talk or understanding seems to reveal the deep structure of reality, including feelings that bind us to (or alienate us from) other people. The feelings aroused by congenial others have a complex effect: feeling safe and valued, we willingly bond to colleagues or friends perceived as stable and trustworthy. Or we, like the escaped prisoner of Plato's cave, imagine that we discern God or the Good as they are. Communities form when

56 COMMUNITY

either condition is satisfied: emotion provokes friendship; compelling interpretations impel religious or ideological bonds.

EMOTION

Hume remarked that "Reason is and ought only to be the slave of the passions."[1] Why is thought subordinate to feeling? Because belief is often pallid without feeling to propel it. Their relation is established when emotion provokes imagination to create idealized or diminished ideas of the persons or situations provoking it: we seek one and flee the other. Locating feeling's origin in the amygdala doesn't explain the diversity of its expressions or their effects on thought and choice; our failure to decipher love, hate, or fear doesn't keep us from acting in ways they determine.

Words are often too blunt for emotion because they fail to distinguish among different feelings (those falling between jealousy and admiration or desire and appreciation), or because they fail to register different intensities of feeling (degrees of fear). Language is more effective when signifying effects such as hostility or care. Aristotle acknowledged three kinds of friendship: respectful, instrumental, and pleasurable. He didn't mention intimacy, though social systems don't exceed their value as utilities until the relations of their members come to be infused with strong feelings and judgments. Jack and Jill meet on a crowded subway when she steps on his foot. They see one another afterward, but their dates are short and polite until they're transformed by mutual affection. *Meaning* (or *significance*)—signifying the complex of feeling, idealization, loyalty, trust, and purpose—is the term that explains them.

INTERPRETATION

Interpretation is significant when it gives us entrée to information that seemed inaccessible: God and his creation or the Good as it makes reality intelligible. Each of these possibilities resembles looking into the sun when the effect is illumination, not blindness. Understanding issues that seemed elusive to finite beings, we disguise our pride when knowing what others resist or haven't learned. For knowledge seems a

Meaning and Normativity

sufficient condition for access: understanding something sublime may be a condition for sheltering within it. Interpretations are, of course, sturdier if true, but reality-testing and truth aren't the critical values if conviction is sufficient for belief.

Community Formation

Communities-of-interest are utilitarian; they form when complementary needs bind people having relevant skills. Communities-of-meaning are more fragile because their formation waits on conditions that are principally psychological.

Emotion or interpretation. Meaning emerges from the emotions aroused when two or more people respond to one another. Affect can go either way: antipathy is repelling, but people bond when feeling support, mutual respect, or attraction. Coming to know one another, they discover practical, aesthetic, intellectual, or moral affinities. Provoked by an issue or problem to which each is sensitive, they agree to an aim, coordinate their roles, and act. Some respond more quickly than others; an opera guild is slower to organize than neighbors fighting a landlord, though both coalesce if feelings are strengthened when focused by a value they share. Yet there needn't be a collateral aim: friendships stabilize when intimacy is all the utility either partner needs. Or the precedent is Plato's cave allegory, where meaning is achieved because interpretation supplies a map of the alleged reality (God or the Good) and a ritual or plan that enables believers to achieve salvation or understanding.[2] People committed to a doctrine are often convinced they've been chosen for a revelation. Sharing the faith is often the emotional force in meaning; it may dominate all they feel or do.

Care. Both interest and meaning are collaborative, though they differ as utility and advantage differ from agents transformed by devotion to one another or to a revered power or idea. Utility asks what needs to be done, then asks what skills are required to do it. The focus in communities-of-meaning is a concern for care, including togetherness, love, or the idealized understandings and aims to which people devote themselves. Emotional attachment may be steady while a community's

58   COMMUNITY

instrumental value is episodic: medical visits are scheduled as needed; family members may care about one another however rarely they meet.

Loyalty and trust. Each partner realizes that his or her relation to the other provokes an expectation: we agree about an aim or task, and the steps to be taken if it's to be realized. You expect me to be your reliable partner in the work required. Our bond is as significant to me as to you: I won't disappoint you. This is solidarity as it converts the strength and intentions of several or many to the purpose of one. Its focus may be pragmatic (a task that's shared), transcendent (we'll go together), or pleasure and support in another's presence.

An idealization. If the aim is worthy, then so is its instrument, the community. (We assume that assembling a community while acquiring appropriate resources violates no significant laws or values.) A community's members idealize their relationship, its aim, and because of their participation, themselves. But this effect isn't the conclusion to an inference; the conviction may be justified by citing reasons or evidence, though its cause is the feeling or interpretation that incites it. The factors provoking community formation differ accordingly. Those of gesellschaft are critical but simple. Meeting someone new is a risk: who is this; what may come of us? People meeting someone of like mind in gemeinschaft expect affinity and accord. Sharing many practices and beliefs, they imagine being supported and led from above. Knowing the other person reduces to learning his or her temperament, interests, and reliability, not what they believe or why they believe it. This difference is crystallized in attitudes to arranged marriages: are they a violation of autonomy or a practice that maximizes likely stability by reducing misunderstanding?

Purpose. Can feeling or interpretation create a relationship without an aim? Friendship may be evidence that it can, mutual support apart. Emphasizing ulterior aims is likely a carryover from the utilities embedded in communities-of-interest. Formed because of interest or need, they thrive when an additional passion—friendship—directs the energy of community members. They're harder to sustain if a community-of-meaning emerged, then dissolved, leaving utility and a salary as their only motives.

Relationships are entities. Members may properly regard their relationships as irreducible to their parts. Members are distinguishable but not separable from the partners to whom they are bonded; their reciprocal causal relations have created this sturdy entity, be it a molecule of atoms, or a friendship. But this is a difficult persuasion in societies where the ontology of individuals and aggregates is an act of faith. Why acknowledge that rabbits are more than collections of rabbit parts? Because the causal relations binding them are as real and functionally decisive as the parts themselves. Why is this claim more than fanciful? Because the relations of the parts are more and other than contiguity and succession, the only relations acknowledged when Hume described causation.[3] Relationships in communities-of-interest and -meaning are those of causal reciprocity, the dynamic established when each affects the other. This is the mechanism responsible for its three engines: reliable continuity and positive and negative feedback. Positive feedback sustains or intensifies the activity enabled by collaboration; each runs faster when bound to a partner running fast. Negative feedback is a brake; quarrels that risk getting out of hand are controlled if each throttles down when seeing the risk to their partnership. Many relationships are effective but only instrumental. This is the sterility alleged against gesellschaft: grateful for efficiency in our many tasks, we don't expect an emotional bond in partnerships that are only utilitarian.

Fellowship

The fellowship appropriate to community is reproof to the idea that it reduces to commonality (as in communities-of-affinity) without meaning/significance: fellowship requires emotional bonds or shared understanding, collaboration, and purpose. The feelings are binding and impelling: we collaborate to achieve aims we share. Here are four examples, each with its signature emotion: (1) family, (2) religion, (3) vocation, and (4) sport.

Family/care. Feelings for one's family and its individual members are too complex for safe generalization. But consider those having one or more parents or caretakers, siblings, grandparents, aunts, uncles, cousins, or those friends who are considered extended family. Why call any such family a community? Because strong feelings locate each member within a tide of history and emotion from which few escape; these are people who will likely be the backdrop to all one is, does, or remembers. Imagine that a crisis befalls one family member while distress floods sensibility in the others. People having no role in this family are uninformed and unconcerned: their indifference speaks to the ways that shared feelings individuate communities while isolating them from one another.

Religion/sanctification. Beliefs and practices differ among religions, but many provoke feelings of sanctification: one is altered, maybe redeemed but also newly calm because relieved of concerns that are more distracting than significant. Religion raises togetherness to effective unity—people sing and pray as one—when emotional intensities sensitize members to resonant cores in one another and themselves.

Vocation/gravitas. Vocations require education, deferred satisfactions, and skills that are regularly challenged by new ideas, techniques, or ambitious colleagues. Every vocation requires a minimum show of competence to convince peers that one has the depth and skill sufficient to earn their respect. Status may require a credential—perhaps a diploma—though specialists know that credentials are a point of entry, not a destination. How is one's work perceived? Fellowship adds resonance, the flow of ideas, and appraisal.

Sport/satisfaction. Athletes are competitive; I can do this better than others have done it, irrespective of who they are or were. Athletes compete with a standard, with one another merely as a point of reference for the standard's current measure. Competitors accept the challenge; training to perfect their skills, they acknowledge and admire those having powers superior to their own. This characterization is focused by individual rather than team sports: tennis or track rather than football. But admiration for one's teammates or opponents is equally strong in them: one admires those who show what power or finesse can be.

Each of these responses has five elements: (1) positive feelings for or about other people; (2) a relationship—community—where the feelings are generated; (3) an idealization of the relationship; (4) loyalty to it; and (5) the intention of seeing one's idealization realized in its context: raising one's child, winning a race.

Idealizations can be reckless or sober. Soaked and trembling in

Meaning and Normativity

a storm, we construe emotion's power as evidence of the angry god causing it. This is imagination as it elides two phases that are better distinguished: first is the inarticulate shock one feels amid an emotional surge; later, thought and language crystallize detail as we describe the experience to others. Theism is an example and a test: do religious communities emerge when people have emotional intimations of the sort described by William James,[4] or does the experience become communicable and "true" only as subjects learn their religion's narrative by hearing its doctrines from socialized members? The story exchanged among them is produced when people wanting to understand and communicate their emotional responses use language to standardize reports of feelings that are otherwise incommunicable. We may assume that the narrative flows naturally from the emotional experience, though the emotions are formless or vague, however strong. The narrative is contrived; enabled by language, it comes later.

The meaning essential to community can now be specified with greater precision. Meaning is emotion or interpretation made significant by the strength of feeling or the purport of the matters conceived. Idealizing either of them tells who I am by virtue of what I feel or believe: Why are you looking so proud? Because that's what I feel when seeing the flag raised. Meaning is socialized because, in the manner of associations, we mirror one another's feelings and aims. The effect is magnetic and propulsive: significant to me because emotionally consequential for both of us, and consequential in itself. The result is a moral contract: we are duty-bound by an idealization and purpose we share because of having promoted it in one another. Reciprocity binds us in meaning, but also in action. For loyalty and purpose, more than sentiment, is the motivational energy in meaning: we who feel its significance are impelled to act, out of regard for one another, on behalf of the aim that binds us. This is community as social agency: people bound by shared meanings organize to achieve their idealized aims.

Communities emerge when meanings are generated and shared by their members, but there are obstacles to success. Loyalty to a community may be strong, belief in its aim or intentional object may be firm. But desire is often frustrated by reality. Solidarity in belief, feeling, and action expresses a community's desire for the existence of something that feeling and imagination aren't sufficient to create:

imagine fans unified by their desire for a home team's victory but unable to will it. We might expect such communities to dissolve for want of evidence that their intentional objects exist, but reverence is sustaining when the bonds of community are stronger than doubts about their likely realization. Yet purpose is not always derailed by frustrated desire. Meaning is often anchored by its intentional objects: friends by one another.

Spirituality. This is a notion sometimes used to elucidate meaning, though its sense is obscure. Does it signify the imagined power—perhaps a god—intimated by an emotion, or merely something consequential but barely intelligible? This uncertainty enables people to defend ideas of transcendence without having to supply independent empirical or logical evidence for whatever condition they infer. The ambiguity is evocative in the lingering attraction for an aspect of gemeinschaft important to those who feel exalted by art or music: is there a transcendent realm of aesthetic values—a god's sensibility—responsible for emotions evoking the sublime?

Some speculations are gratuitous, but discipline is hard to learn because our societies escaped only recently from the persuasion that everything has its explanation in a god's powers. The transcendentalism evoked by emotion isn't irrational if it intimates our sense that reality—in art, nature, history, or society—stretches beyond us. Yet their scale may be all we legitimately infer when evoking something vast or numinous. Nor is anything more required: sensibility in art or music is sufficiently explained by things seen or heard and the cultivation that makes us responsive.

Solidarity. Meaning is the difference when communities-of-meaning emerge from utilitarian social systems. Are those systems changed in any significant way by the feelings and idealizations that meanings comprise? Practical systems are goal directed; they work efficiently if skilled role-players perform as competent leaders prescribe. Emotion isn't absent because members may feel considerable satisfaction in the work they do or their way of doing it. But there may be no emotional commitment to the system, its aim, or to one another, given a salary and benefits. Meaning of a kind is present because specialists feel pleasure when testing their vocational skills, yet members who work well together may be devoid of fellow feeling, hence of loyalty to one another and their system. Think of local transport, hospitals, armies, and airlines, all organized to serve people of many kinds. Labor turnover is constant as workers take other jobs with no commitment to any employer beyond the duties specified in their contracts. These systems cohere because of their design, leadership, and worker skills, but they lack the intrinsic glue, the idealization, purpose, and feeling that establish communities-of-meaning.

Karl Marx believed that community would enhance labor's ability to improve workers' lives. He invoked meaning as interpretation when labor's objective condition—workers driving down salaries by competing with one another—was distinguished from the solidarity to be achieved by realizing that competition enfeebles their bargaining power with management. Workers would become partners empowered by an aim.[5] Why do agents believe in the aims their communities prescribe? Sometimes, because purpose is captive to socialized habits and beliefs; more thoughtfully, because they rightly suppose that collaboration is a necessary condition for the effective mobilization of their powers. Loyalty and consensus are vulnerable to corrupt or misguided leaders—trust is sometimes betrayed—but that's a problem for vigilant oversight, not a fault in community. But, you say, communities are debased by the bad faith of some members. That's true, but no more a deficiency in community than health is qualified by the risk of disease.

Sentiment. Saying that communities form when the role-players of utilities come to have feelings for one another and their system seems to imply that community supplements efficacy with sentiment. That persuasion ignores idealization, intention, and their effects on motivation. Look to see which social systems are effective: one likely finds good leadership and design, able workers, and sufficient resources. Communities are distinguished by something additional. Start from simple examples—family and friendship—to see that meaning distinguishes relationships that are principally or only utilitarian from those impelled by shared feelings and idealization. This difference is never less than implicit in Rousseau's *Social Contract*, where he describes people leaving the state of nature for the interdependence of civil society. It distinguishes the Public, people organized for self-regulation, from the Great Community, citizens joined by civic and moral sentiments, in Dewey's *The Public and Its Problems*. One might believe that community so conceived is more an intellectual abstraction than a social power, but Dewey hoped to unify moral sentiment with civic pride: citizens would embody republican ideals and act accordingly. Obstacles would form, but we would continue the project of creating a perfected republic. That was decades before January 6, 2021 proved that America hadn't coalesced.

Univocity. A different uncertainty is more easily resolved: why suppose that a community's members agree about the character of the meanings that join them, given their origins in feeling and understanding? Available markers in physiology and behavior may be identical for any two of a community's members without confirming that their emotional or interpretive experiences are qualitatively the same. Yet feelings or thoughts needn't be alike to confirm sameness of meaning if emotion or understanding provokes an intention and behavior appropriate to a shared aim. Purpose is the common denominator; its control is manifest in the ways a community responds to its circumstances: businesses organize to sell, schools to teach. But here, too, ambiguity is acceptable: emotions provoking allegiance to a monarch may fixate on the royal family, its palace, or an anthem. Intention in a context supersedes these variations: what does a community intend, then what does it do?

Meanings that begin in feeling or interpretation incite purpose, then the passion that drives purpose to its aim. Actions consistent with purpose are, therefore, a test of intention. What do you say, what do you mean? Do you plan or believe or wish? Prove it by showing what you do. Praying, parenting, or working with one's mates reliably fixes one's intention in members' eyes. Yet this isn't the final word, because irresolution betrays idealization, or because complexity or lack of resources makes a task unmanageable. Community dissolves, because skill and intention are misaligned.

Normativity

Communities are normative because of the causal reciprocities and meanings that establish and sustain them.

Reciprocity. Reciprocity is normative because the interactions of a dynamical system's constituents are stabilized by negative feedback. Imagine a buzzer that alerts drivers when their cars go too slow for traffic or too fast for safety. But why suppose that speedometers are reliable? Because they're built to specific tolerances, and work as designed. The complementarity of designs is the explanation for reliable effects, hence normativity in all of industry and biology. Yet this solution isn't definitive because the first question is subsumed by another: why assume—the problem of induction—that the future will be like the past? We don't have better answers than those of Aristotle and Descartes: Aristotle as he observed that effects are reliable when kinds of things mesh predictably;[6] Descartes as he reduced Aristotle's substantial forms (qualitative kinds) to the variables of geometry.[7] So, the pieces of a jigsaw puzzle fit one another because of their complementary shapes. Add velocity and the topology of space-time to its geometry, stipulate their stability, and we explain the normativity of geometrized motion in space-time, now and in the future.

Yet this solution is remote from the emergent orders—whether natural or conventional—of social relations. Reciprocities that are core, transactional, or holistic are embedded in webs of rules. Each sector is interwoven or overlaid with others, while known for virtues that distinguish it: affection for core relations; honesty and efficiency for those transactional; loyalty and deference for the reciprocities of states and religions. Each has inhibitions regulating negative feedback, and spurs that provoke its positive version: responsibility and pleasure in the case of core reciprocities; tasks and satisfaction when relations are transactional; stability when holistic feedback is negative; justice or salvation when it's positive. Duty is the invariant normative demand; habit is its reliable ground. Placed in situations requiring a skill and promising a reward, we perform. Habits, in themselves, are normative, yet some roles demand the conscious focus one brings to difficult tasks;

66   COMMUNITY

those performed under the aegis of meaning are enabled by affection for our partners or by shared understandings. Participants regulate themselves—negative feedback—by acting as their roles require when disruptive inclinations would subvert aims and reciprocities that maintain viable relations. Positive feedback looks the other way: pleasure and satisfaction stabilize reciprocities within the viable parameters where role-players are mutually engaged.

We don't yet know how to explain everything by citing its material constituents or conditions; it is, so far, only a grand surmise that all of it is explicable in those terms. Discussion proceeds in the meantime by lurching back and forth between cogent observations of practical life and the speculative frontiers of physics. The normativities of practical life are, for example, comprehensible without regard for information more arcane than observation makes available. So, agents enter reciprocities knowing their rules: buying a newspaper requires paying for it; making a date for lunch requires arriving at the chosen time and place. There would be no reciprocities, or none that occur reliably, without norms that regulate conduct; why make oneself vulnerable to cost and effort if there is no shared understanding that reciprocity is a commitment to perform in the way agreed? The perpetual buzz of social activity is the foreground signifying our shared assumptions; they establish the weave of responsibilities stored in the sustaining rules and expectations of myriad situations. What produced them? They accrete over generations of interdependence as agents learn the conditions for collaborations having sustainable and desired effects. Other norms were possible, but we formalize these after appraising their effects.

Most norms are learned as children educated in the ways of their culture. Adults take them for granted; they're a comfortable backdrop to all we do. Other tribes do something similar because styles of cooperation are common to all cultures before being refined for histories, specialized tasks, and rules native to some. But many others—instrumental functions, especially—depend for their survival on local networks of supporting systems. Families need work, housing, schools, health care, and companions. Their schools need teacher training, public or private funding, students, and sponsors. Some of a network's agencies may not rise to the demands of community—personal intensity and care, for

MEANING AND NORMATIVITY

example—but several or many do. For every community-of-interest or -meaning has needs others satisfy or share. One may imagine the dominating communities of old as they purged or subordinated every competitor, but that image is wrong in the flat social topography where interdependence is the norm.

A team's players have roles and rules to satisfy if their team is to win, but that isn't true of its fans: hence the implication that each of a network's systems may have distinctive tasks and values in a mix of roles that enrich it for all. Complexity emerges, various interests are satisfied when the isolated houses of rude settlements mature as webs of stores, homes, and schools. But is there normativity in these evolving ensembles; is each a community stabilized by its norms? There is self-control and mutual aid because residents want the safety and security of peaceable relations to other residents. This is a glimmer of community, but not enough to explain a network of local relations, many or most that are anonymous or assumed: grateful for the people who stock the local supermarket, I don't know them, local police, sanitation workers, or the local city councilwoman. One doesn't create a totalizing community of people emotionally responsive to one another merely by taking care not to damage the links of reliable interdependence. That additional step requires the integration of its interdependent systems, plus the reliable cooperation of their members.

Dewey's idea of the public, like those of Kant and Mill, founded community in republican meanings: community as mutual tolerance and respect. This is a condition for the personal autonomy we have learned to want, but their idea of gesellschaft's reciprocities is too cerebral, too abstract for most people.

Meaning. Social phenomena are not yet reducible to the simplest variables of physics, relations included. Their normativity doesn't map well onto constraints intrinsic to a geometrized space-time. Yet meaning is normative in several ways: (1) feelings are normative because intention fixes their referents—one is angry at something or someone, anger may cool without deflecting its intention; (2) meanings provoke actions intended to satisfy an idealization—having valorized feelings guides one's behavior; and (3) We hold one another to shared intentions because satisfying them requires collaboration. People who share a

68 COMMUNITY

meaning (a feeling, idealization, and purpose) anticipate that partners will act accordingly; knowing one another's expectation, they satisfy it. The causal reciprocities of utilitarian systems exhibit this convergence.

Socializing an aim is an efficient way of promoting the habits, feelings, and understanding that facilitate utility: we care for the sick because of sympathy for their pain, and recognition that all of us are vulnerable. Yet this justification is insufficient when preferred norms diverge. Which is decisive: a community's commitment to the health of its members or the crises of members needing medicine or a blood transfusion? Emotion and interpretations are obstacles when both sides justify their responses by citing what they believe to be the overriding meanings.

Governance. Normativity of a different kind is imposed by rules or laws that discipline the beliefs, feelings, and practices of a community's members. This is governance; it has three forms. One that's personal is founded in habits, values, and intentions. Another crystallizes piecemeal within social activities as people and their systems—schools, teams, or families—standardize practices and their constitutive reciprocities in ways calculated to maximize efficacy while minimizing friction. The third is holistic oversight: laws, the police, and courts. Communities require all three: self-disciplined role-players; a playing field in which communities pursue their aims with minimal interference; and regulation that anticipates conflict or intervenes to stop it.

This layering is manifest in gemeinschaft, when every region and part is regulated in ways fixed by the whole. It seems unreasonable to gemeinschaft's defenders that humans, so little capable of controlling their impulses, could reliably rule themselves, though pluralist, pragmatic societies are no less committed to order. The difference between them is the seat of the regulator: a state or religion or the prudence and self-control of individuals and their systems. Gesellschaft societies have three priorities: freedom, efficacy, and innovation. Each is sanctioned by long-established sentiments or understandings: freedom enables self-discovery, initiative, and invention; order stills the fear of disruption; innovation averts stasis or transforms a frontier.

Pious societies satisfy this essay's criterion for community, but democrats satisfy it, too: these persuasions are joined in communities that satisfy socially accepted aims while respectful of members and those they affect. Orientation distinguishes disciplinary spaces of the two kinds: from the bottom up in gesellschaft, where rules are responses to conflict or coagulation, but top down when gemeinschaft's edicts determine what can or can't be done. Equivocation is always apparent because reality doesn't align perfectly with idealized disciplinary spaces. Traffic laws in Jerusalem and Rome were established by their pragmatic municipalities, not by religious authorities.

A logical test. It may be objected that neither causal reciprocity nor meaning is normative: both may be impelled by habit or intention but neither satisfies the demand that no judgment or assertion is normative unless its negation is a contradiction. This is a test of necessary truths, those obtaining in every possible world. Most are trivial and indifferent to the practical and moral contingencies that emerge when people collaborate for safety or well-being. These origins are local and maybe unique; they explain and justify cultural norms—those of diet or dress—having meaning as their rationale, and normativity as the mark of good practice. Their standards are the sediments of histories that could have been different; they don't imply meaning's global determination of social norms, but neither do they seem contingent to people humiliated if they're breached.

Discounting normativities local to a time or place is a retreat into the intellectual empyrean where universalizing abstraction trumps practice and need. It ignores the times when a singularity—construction and operation of the James Webb telescope—exemplifies normativity in practical life. Why doesn't ordinary usage distinguish more systematically between the two uses: one implying universality and necessity, another implying the rigor of effective collaboration? Perhaps because context is sufficient to distinguish them; or because Hume, after Descartes, assumed that nothing is necessary if its negation is not a contradiction. That leaves the normativities of nature and practical life unexplained. Are they merely conventional or accidental?

Is and must. Normativity—the distinction between *is* and *ought* or *is* and *must*—introduces binocular modal vision into our perception of things: seeing them as they are, we also discern what they should be. Distinguishing the two makes us responsible for remaking one to the design of the other. Our norms are often fantasies, unrealized and unrealizable. But some of what is determines what more there should

70 COMMUNITY

be. When possibility is material as well as logical, communities are likely the causes making the possible actual.

Utilities alone might have that effect, though meaning and community are also its enablers: meaning because the idealizations it provokes tell us what to do, communities-of-meaning because they enable doing those things when altruistic aims exceed basic needs. This is meaning and value as they penetrate and condition utility: we do more than practical life requires because idealization has spoken in each of us before circumstances have made us sober.

Mill acknowledged that asocial people sometimes socialize (*On Liberty*'s third region of liberty);[8] he realized (in *Utilitarianism*) that individuality is achieved as moral autonomy when people choose the duties of community.[9] Reciprocity and duty are, this implies, as elemental as freedom. How are freedom and duty reconciled? That happens when interests and needs make us interdependent; collaboration is seamless if meaning enables accord. This response may explain the sense of transcendence experienced when feelings and beliefs are synchronized among people who share an aim. But there is a risk: are we practical and hard to fool or easily controlled by people or communities that promise enlightenment, salvation, or easy access to mythology?

There is also this lingering issue: is it significant that human communities require meanings shared among cooperators, whereas ants and bees coordinate their actions without them? For it isn't likely that bugs cooperate because of shared idealizations or intentions, if hardwiring enables their collaborations. But is that all? Could they be stirred by an effect comparable to emotion's effects in us? This is the difference between cars safely aligned on highways because of an algorithm responsible for distributing them, and the same effect occurring when prudent drivers establish safe distances between themselves and cars they follow. There may be no current information sufficient to decide which it is.

Ambivalence

Gemeinschaft and gesellschaft have contrary implications for meaning and normativity. Meaning in this dispute emphasizes interpretation

Meaning and Normativity

rather than feeling: do we construe ourselves as formed within a totalizing society or free to enjoy relationships of our choosing in places congenial to our beliefs and tastes? We like order, stability, and the idea of togetherness, but holism is vulnerable to the religious or monarchic absolutism rejected by the Enlightenment. Hostile to authoritarian cultures, we prefer the risks implied by contingency, the open spaces of gesellschaft to the plenum of gemeinschaft.

These are the two sides of an ancient quarrel: essentialist, on one side, existentialist, on the other. Should babies be swaddled or loosely clothed—forced to accommodate to the rigid forms encasing them or free to move as they choose? Which characterization best represents us: we're formed by the social order in which we're born and educated, or we form the social space we occupy in ways determined by our choice of partners, tasks, and aims? These possibilities mark the extremes. (There is also this third possibility: the situation of people having no secure set of places or understandings in which to locate themselves, and neither powers nor resources for determining the rules governing their choices and actions.)

We're of two minds: security and significance or opportunity and initiative. We romanticize the well-being community once implied while insisting on our freedom to do as we please. Life in autocratic regimes may have little romance or meaning: the effects of overwhelming power used arbitrarily intimidate people without endearing local enforcers. Religion's effects are better received because the idea that a just and rational god presides over nature and humanity is credible to many people. Organized religions are respected as their god's intermediaries; their practices are accepted ways of submitting to a god's authority while earning a personal dispensation for the observant. When all but a few were believers, meaning was critical evidence of one's faith. Its rituals seemed obligatory to believers confident that their practices and prayers were divinely authorized. One could explain one's faith by repeating a narrative that invoked each of its constituent factors: emotion, idealization, loyalty, and purpose. Houses of worship were perceived as holy spaces; congregants reasonably supposed that they were more plainly visible to their god because closer to him when present there. One could explain it by repeating a narrative that invoked each factor.

People still feel this aura and its promise, though society at large has dismantled the assumptions and social structures it required. The change began centuries ago, though believers are still captive to meanings and actions that enhance their imagined well-being by proving their worth in the eyes of their god. Why is that a common motive? Where answers should have plausibility and depth, these two may be too simple: (1) We're curious—What could the universe be? How was it created? Why is there something rather than nothing? Uncertain in all these respects but quick to imagine, we assume the truth of our speculations. (2) We are incidental to the cosmos, and to many of our relationships and circumstances. Knowing our vulnerability, wanting more, we imagine being saved because our worth is acknowledged.

God and the Good are economical answers to both issues: believing our religious or ideological speculations locates us within a closed world while reconciling us to mysteries excused because their scale is so much grander than our understanding. Why trust in faith? Because the idealization meaningful to many others is meaningful to me; I would be less confident of my beliefs if everyone else disdained them. But they don't; they're ardent: singing, praying together expresses meanings and resolve we share. The order I discern in nature, like the worth I perceive in others, implies duties and norms I require of myself. I am situated amid complexities having a purpose and design. Knowing their creator, I am comfortable in them and myself. I could be embarrassed by the frailty that makes me credulous, though weakness looks like strength when a tide of believers obscures the anxiety we share. This is gemeinschaft: totalizing community and its meanings makes me whole.

Gesellschaft starts in autonomy and evolves from there: who and where am I if talk of a god, and the fixed morals and roles over which it presides are a fantasy? Gesellschaft's moderate expressions emphasize choice and coherence: assemble an array of systems and act in ways likely to stabilize them and oneself. But there is also a more extreme version: imagine yourself in situations where circumstances enable you and others to reinvent principal modes of production or other life-sustaining activities. Exploit an unforeseen technology to drive social arrangements in ways unforeseen. Create the understandings and

Meaning and Normativity

rules that will make them intelligible to other people; let them learn new rules and expectations.

Normativity is intellectually obscure, but experientially vivid: we don't cross busy streets against red lights or expect soft landings when jumping from high places. Nature's laws are determinable but unforgiving when violated; they may be satisfied in many ways within variable ranges of values, but not in every way. Seeing the regularities in practical life, we explain them by saying that devices are more likely to be reliable if they're well made. That explanation works, too, for as much of normativity and behavior as we understand: the changes tolerable to gesellschaft societies are likely to be incremental, however quick. It will be a while before there are postcards from Mars, or societies where the police are defunded because no one breaks the law.

Ideologies are usually not developed sufficiently to specify norms that are more than rules. Marx's version of communism is different because his idea of dialectical materialism revealed, he supposed, the developmental law of social process.[10] Starting in the distributed powers of medieval landowners, the law was said to drive the consolidation of wealth through epochs of ocean trade and factory production to the time when industrial power would pit capitalist owners against organized labor. Their conflict would end in labor's control of factories, capital, and state power; the end was forceable because necessary. It would come, Marx supposed, because workers would discover their need for solidarity; mutual esteem would bind them when communal spirit was compensation for sacrifices (in salary or working conditions) that each worker might need to make for the sake of their cause. Other ideas of social normativity—those of Adam Smith, for example—were regulative but conventional: cultivate virtue; prevent damage to open markets by averting the collusion of a market's dominant financial powers. We were to generate community by voluntarily submitting to prudent regulation.

Theologians, more than legislators or economists, are likely to be communitarians with realist views of normativity. They would have us believe that nature has a design, and that its norms, moral or material, are God's laws. The theology underlying some religious versions of gemeinschaft is starkly normative when it postulates hierarchically

74 COMMUNITY

ordered modes of reality: God, the necessary being; angels whose existence is eternal though contingent on God's will; and the mortals whose finite existence is a contingency sustained by God.[11] Where beings of these kinds are categorially distinct, their realms of being are closed to one another; norms appropriate to one have no application in the other two. People learning of these ontological barriers aren't surprised by political, social, and economic barriers that seem equally firm. Where social space is conceived as a plenum, occupied and differentiated by tribes, classes, or people having disparate degrees of authority, they accept the places and roles assigned them. *Freedom*, in their context, signifies the power and opportunity to satisfy roles one inherits or acquires.

Religious communities that share this ontological persuasion may interpret it in either of two ways: they're elated by their God's creative act and their preference in his eyes, or terrified by his remorseless power. Meanings gravitate either way: community members like one another while proud of their significance to God, or they bond for consolation when fearful of his judgments. *Gemeinschaft* is solace in either case for those wanting the secure identity—hence rights and duties—that comes with life in an established order. This cosseted state, like gender relations in traditional societies, is attractive to people who fear isolation or defeat in the open spaces where gesellschaft promises the freedom to make an identity and place of one's own. Gemeinschaft postulates an immobile grid of hierarchical relations, one fully structured by the ontological differences of its contents; relations in the Leibnizian spaces favored by gesellschaft are structured by the relative and changing velocities, aims, and positions of their occupants.[12]

Systems in the spaces of gemeinschaft may have either or both of two bases: many are communities-of-interest; some—families and friendships—are bound by the emotions, idealizations, and loyalties of their members. These are idealized as sanctuaries—intermediaries between the infinite whole and its finite parts—that bring the moral force of the whole to the lives of its communicants. The communities of gesellschaft are more fragile because they lack the ontological normativity of Thomistic realms of being. (Meaning is critical to the com-

Meaning and Normativity

munities-of-interest or -meaning formed in Leibnizian spaces because it, along with need and interest, directs their formation.) Few natural roles mediate between these alternatives, though friendship and family encourage the formation of community networks in the neighborhoods, businesses, and schools of gesellschaft societies.

Gesellschaft communities—families and friendships apart—are alliances, not the zones to which we retreat for meaning and comfort. Formed with an eye to possible advantages, they're hard to maintain when members imagine doing better for themselves by doing something else. Temporary affiliations, each with its emotional rise, suit us better when nothing may be permanent. Yet freedom from authority and fixed places exempts us from interference without telling us what we could effectively do or be. That requires a direction and resources for which we are personally responsible, though we're vulnerable in environments where no social structures—no safety nets—defend us or establish stable personal identities. Hence our anxiety and the recourse in sentiment to holistic communities—to gemeinschaft societies—that are no longer plausible or available to most of us.

Our ambivalence—open to opportunity or settled and secure—is besetting because unresolvable. Gemeinschaft looks backward to relationships crafted to fill established places in the web of God's creation. Perceiving only a local piece of the design, its loyalists are grateful for meanings that bind them to neighbors. Others breathe more freely in open spaces or frontiers; they enjoy the company of friends, but maybe not too many all at once. Their communities are smaller than the global churches of gemeinschaft where individuality often reduces to instances of a type because all conform to the beliefs and practices of their faith. Normativity in gesellschaft is founded in the constitutive causal relations of their members and in the laws or rules improvised to regulate communities and other social relations. The only global regulations acknowledged are the minimal constraints required to maximize freedom of movement while minimizing harm in the social spaces where communities assemble.

Most people don't fall on either end of this contrariety; some are steadfast in closed communities of God or the Good, others thrive in open societies where initiative creates work and norms in what seemed

76 COMMUNITY

a void. The Great Community for many is an incantation, regret for opportunities they never had.

Two Kinds of Morality

Gemeinschaft encourages morality of a kind that's osmotic: one is coupled to a community's other members in belief and practice. Singing or praying with them, we're warmed by their proximity; faith is confirmed by the intensity all may feel. Gesellschaft prefers judgment to prescription or osmosis as the basis for moral choice. Its version of morality requires education and deliberation: education because information is critical to judgment; deliberation because weighing one's options is critical to the likely viability of one's choices. But situations vary; agents considering the same circumstances will come to different conclusions about the right or effective thing to do. The diversity of judgments requires conversations about the better way to proceed.

Gemeinschaft declares its interventions moral when its principles are deployed. Its agents likely "know" what to do; those of gesellschaft make a choice, then move ahead while sensitive to likely obstacles. This difference is notable in practical life where dicta for raising children or running businesses compete with practical rules garnered over time and experience. Gesellschaft's agents think consequentially and act on judgments that are tentative to some degree. Yet there is stability because fine-tuning in diverse situations generates rules that are widely acceptable, save for exceptional times.[13] This emphasis on the variability of situations is decried by moral absolutists. They dislike its plasticity, finding that it comes with too many values subject to qualification or compromise, and it provides no firm basis for deciding any moral issue. But this is excessive: knowing our needs and vulnerabilities, sensitive to the history of situations like most of those at hand, we have plausible rules and procedures. Situations and perspectives vary; but we can and do make cogent moral judgments within the range of tolerable variations, given our vulnerability to circumstances and possibilities unknown.

Communities exhibit these contrary orientations: some settle comfortably in routines that make them predictably effective; others seem tentative or befuddled. But this can be true whether the context is gemeinschaft or gesellschaft: marriages and businesses can be more or less stable in either. The difference between them is the degree of security that each imparts to its communities. Gemeinschaft projects conviction: marry on its terms and one knows the course ahead. Gesellschaft may be unsettling: people joined in its space know that their futures will be shaped by contingencies they can't predict.

Notice that moral ascriptions extend beyond community members to communities themselves. Individual morality is derivative in communities founded by a god or embodying the good; one of gemeinschaft's justifications is the ease with which it explains the demands on personal virtue by locating individuals within global communities where intentions and conduct are shaped by the origin or purpose of the whole. Gesellschaft seems weaker because the morality it describes emerges as people collaborate to satisfy shared or complementary interests. A functioning community is evidence that there is consensus among its members about the attitudes and rules appropriate to its aims.

Duties

More than willing to help partners, community members feel a duty to one another and to their system. Duty is a psychological impulse—an enduring sense of commitment to others—before being reified in deontological space (the space of norms and duties). Duty evolves in stages: first, as people have expectations about their forming relationships; later, as partners have roles within the causal reciprocities binding them to others (do as you say or imply you'll do); finally, as one acts to satisfy their expectations. Duties fulfilled are the culminating expressions of trust. Each partner makes core demands to which responses have become habitual. One doesn't have to think about availability to a spouse or friend, though the intensities binding a community's members vary through a spectrum of loyalties: to one's child, neighbor, or the Long Island Ducks. Communities of different strengths are the stable result: the intense personal relationships of traditional communities compare to the sporadic contacts of cities, where tasks and autonomy dominate intimacy and meaning.

Duties form in the intensities of the practices that satisfy interests and needs; their formation is prior to the formulation of the laws making their satisfaction incumbent. Mill rightly supposed that morality begins in the relationships and expectations of people going about their daily lives. Critics object that a practice isn't desirable because it's desired, but Mill wouldn't have thought it is. We discredit the established relationships of sadists and their willing victims by remarking that rules and practices aren't moral unless they satisfy two tests: rules established over a succession of practical trials must enhance the well-being of those affected. Universal measures of well-being are contested; there may be, we acknowledge, exceptions to any rule or practice.

Laws that formalize one's duties, with costs for ignoring them, are a defense against those who ignore responsibilities they've chosen or inherited. Those are principles regularly invoked in courts, though the number of such occasions is meager relative to those satisfied by committed partners. Yet duties are sometimes problematic because one participates in communities (whether utilities or those of meaning) having conflicting aims or schedules: How is one to be in two places at once? How is a resource to be used for one task without precluding its use for another? There are also times when there is uncertainty about the person benefiting from duty's satisfaction: Can duty to oneself override duties to others, and if so, when and why? Is autonomy always a power for satisfying duties to others, or is it sometimes a power for fulfilling an idea of oneself?

The web of rules and laws is a patchwork quilt of accommodations to local stresses or conflicts, plus a grid of proscriptions deemed appropriate for all occasions. Kantian deontology introduces its simplifying rule: don't will a maxim that prescribes appropriate behavior unless any (every) agent in your circumstances could will it without contradiction. This strategy expressed Kant's belief that a universalizing logic would cut through the thicket of conventional laws and practices. No one could successfully lie if none believed others; commerce would suffocate if none offered credit because debtors refuse to pay their bills. Yet Kant's procedure has nothing to say about swathes of moral life where generalization isn't plausible: to whom is one duty bound for help when one can't help everyone? No one? The justification for helping someone preferred isn't universalizable because one's resources are smaller than the need and because one has no access to most of the needy.

Kant's ethics provides no direction when universalizing doesn't generate contradictions, though we are regularly obliged to choose and act. Mill's principle is closer to the guidance required when choosing what to do: do no harm. Feed those for whom you're responsible, while encouraging others to do the same. Acknowledge that there are some things none should do, while recognizing that there seem to be no simple rubrics that unravel tortured moral complexities: what's to be done when several are hungry, though there is only enough to feed one. What would Kant have us do? He chastises benevolence for the want of universality, but which practice or principle is preferable when resources and opportunities are finite while, as often happens, universalizing fails to direct us in situations at hand: How does one give apples to all when there are only ten apples but many more to feed? Or is this a reminder that Kant was a libertarian, whose principal moral concern was a rule sufficient to avert sabotage to the framework of a society's moral practices—don't lie, pay creditors—when the complexity of needs versus resources has no a priori fix?

More challenging to him is the suspicion that morality is often irreducibly situational: is it plain that some of the imperative's violations (lying, stealing, killing) are never moral? Might there be laws or principles other than the categorical imperative having force that's universal, but loose? Are there natural moral laws, each a constraint that reveals and ranks one's duties to others and oneself? They're inferred after observing nature's ebb and flow: how high or low can a value (truth-telling or lying) go before a practice loses viability? Situational ethics, like all empirical inquiries, is slow and fallible, but it promises a deeper understanding of rules that apply, mostly, across human practice. It requires judgments and choices. Rules crystallize from them.

Moral Orientations

Religions and ideologies are static—they embody "truths" that are slow to change—though rigidity makes their communities fragile when people organize for newly discovered aims or means. Gemeinschaft communities are stockades when defensive and ferocious; converts may prayerfully enter; no one should leave. Benign versions are conceivable, but that isn't always their history. The members of gesellschaft communities—whether communities-of-interest, -meaning, or -at-large—orient themselves in either of nine ways.

Out of respect for the community. Participating in gesellschaft communities requires that one accept their terms: someone wanting his or her roles and identity fixed by a holistic regime will be disappointed by having to make the choices that decide it. There is also this intermediate condition: float in social currents while able to choose or until it's too late to make choices one prefers.

In response to an idea or feeling. We can choose what to do and with whom because of shared interests or a rush of feelings. But are we autonomous—free to choose—when impelled by feeling? Gemeinschaft regimes encourage us to trust the choices of authorities; gesellschaft requires that we be disciplined by inhibition and judgment.

Out of commitment to the community's aim. What is proposed; why do it? The response to an offer or inclination may be emotional or intellectual. We participate because the aim is worthy (irrespective of personal advantage).

Out of devotion to a vital role. Some tasks demand rare skills, some (difficult surgeries) that aren't viable without the support of specialized teams. Devotion to a community may express one's gratitude for the opportunity it provides.

Because one's skills are challenged by the task proposed. People who enjoy an activity are glad to show what they can do.

Out of regard for other members. One might have joined an unknown community at the invitation of a friend. But then duties to its members becomes the motive sustaining one's commitment.

Out of regard for its meaning. Members may explain themselves by saying without elaboration, "Much that I do is humdrum, but this is meaningful." Other goods—practical benefits—may seem less relevant.

Out of regard for the effects on nonparticipants. Playing in a fine orchestra is confirmation of one's skill; playing before an appreciative audience is an additional incentive. But what if music played in an open-air concert is noise to other ears? One doesn't abstain from playing if the effects on them are mildly annoying, though who decides the degree of harm: those responsible for an effect or those who suffer it? The two sides negotiate: we'll play before or after dinner, not when you're asleep.

Because of fearing the costs of leaving a community or resisting its demands. Community membership is a contingency that works better for some than for others. Participants know that leaving a family or job is likely disruptive or destructive to the system, other members, or oneself. But is the distress so severe that one hesitates to go, or does going promise liberation from a greater pain? One may not know.

The variety of these measures make it likely that any two of a community's members may find communication difficult because differences in their respective commitments and roles are belied by the uniformity of their behavior. We'd rather not know that the moral persuasions of people close to us are different from our own. Gemeinschaft settles the issue by declaring its principles, though no formula resolves these uncertainties in gesellschaft societies. Is there, nevertheless, a way that participants can make their scruples known to one another? One way is the inhibition that deters us when we don't know the way forward, then more generally one's observations of what others do or decline. Situations are always particular and often complex; they change unpredictably, so one makes choices in ambiguous situations.

What's to be expected when agents with different moral profiles find themselves bound to one another within a system's reciprocally related roles: a marriage, for example? Their aim may be nominally similar, though their ideas about achieving it may be morally different. Martin Buber, Kant, and Immanuel Levinas thought it critical that partners perceive and relate to one another as ends, not means; they would emphasize that behavior appropriate to a role is distinct from taking care that the role's task doesn't distract from the personhood of those it affects. The Mill of *On Liberty* was careless on this point: he seems to have regarded social "unities" as having instrumental value only: "[F]rom the liberty of each individual follows the liberty, within the same limits, of combination among individuals; freedom to unite for any purpose not involving harm to others; the persons combining being supposed to be of full age and not forced or deceived."[14] One joins utilities—giving help to get it—because one can't satisfy an aim or need without help. Partners, this implies, are distinguished by their skills, not by qualities or identities that would make them notable in themselves (though concern for a partner's vulnerability and worth are the core of moral duty in Mill's *Utilitarianism*). But this leaves a vital question unanswered: do we appraise our partners by considering what they do, or by searching for evidence of their intentions? Performance rules—norms less severe than imperatives (their negations aren't contradictions)—control an agent's response to a role: satisfy the task that defines it. (I'm a plumber, you say, here to provide the help for which you called. I'll show you the moral side of me by what I do, not by encouraging you to discern my sympathies or intentions.)

Two additional issues are implied but unconsidered: what is one to do when experience shows that an apparently shared aim can't be achieved because the scruples of a community's other members differ from one's own? Compromise is the solution often commended, though intentions may not be susceptible to accommodation. The more appropriate response may be divorce. The other question lingers in the space contested by gemeinschaft and gesellschaft: are there doctrines so comprehensive or rules so deep that every moral issue is settled by consulting them? Gemeinschaft societies simplify teaching and learning by assuming that this is so. Is that because holistic doctrines are infinitely subtle, or because we put our faith in the judgment of authoritarian rulers? We may believe that Kant also proposed general solutions for any moral issues—ask if a maxim can be generalized without contradiction—but Kant's ethics solves only those cases where choice and action are inhibited because a contradiction would be entailed (no one would believe anyone if all were to lie). Kant has no solution for the many cases where no contradiction results from choosing and acting on a maxim. Those are situations where choice is directed by sensibility and fallible judgments, not logic. This result—irresolution—explains the indecision that sweeps through gesellschaft societies when there is no accord about the moral solution for issues that arise.

Moral Identity

Societies organized in the style of gemeinschaft are conservative: normative relations are fixed by tradition; members are likely to have generic identities appropriate to their roles. Members' privacies may be an array of dark holes, invisible and unknown, though mutual recognition is easy when generic identities—mother, father, policeman, priest—are fixtures in communities they form or inherit. Gesellschaft is different because people are transparent to the degree that they are known to those seeing the choices they make. Identity is transformed: before it was a role; now it's the power to choose, satisfy, and integrate one's roles.

Gesellschaft's agents create arrays of microcommunities centered by the individuals—the nodes—responsible for their assembly and stability. Agents' intentions and partners' expectations control choices and actions within the circles of these relationships. Norms they establish are standardized because needs, resources, and available utilities are common to many or all. A *gemeinschaft* that's loose and accommodating may have subaltern communities similar to those of a pluralist society, because members value parents, teachers, and reliable collaborators. It sometimes matters less that one is formed in a society that's tolerant or traditional. The paradigms converge because people living in societies of both kinds need family, education, safety, and work. Yet those acquiring moral form in gemeinschaft's supportive space are less likely to sustain it in circumstances that are disrupted or morally indifferent; people who learned a norm while making their way in morally formless circumstances may remember it better. Compare skilled cooks, disoriented when deprived of a well-equipped kitchen, to those who make something rare with only a saucepan.

Is this a difference in the powers of moral identity or a measure of their enabling contexts: gemeinschaft or gesellschaft? It's both, because moral identity is a function of the several factors determining character's development: the inclinations, understandings, and habits shaped by personal experience, and the community-of-accord in which character forms. Gemeinschaft is rigid; gesellschaft is permissive. One prescribes the shapes of acceptable characters; the other encourages experiments that discover form or create it. Yet the good or bad parent,

84   COMMUNITY

teacher, or friend is similar in both. Today's versions of gesellschaft are more constraining than Tönnies imagined; gemeinschaft's expressions are less so. One tolerates experiments; the other expects them. Actions are, however, appraised more harshly in purist communities-of-accord: has one acquired moral identity by following its recipes, or by engaging other children while observing nearby adults? Church and school, or play?

Where is the evidence for the surmise that societies elide despite the contrariety of their paradigms? *First* is the decline of global communities, whether ideological or religious, and the ruptured verticality—the hierarchies—that bind people in stratified roles, fixed beliefs and practices. *Second* is the horizontal complexity of secular life, the reciprocities binding each person to several or many others for disparate tasks and aims. *Third* is the variety of our choices; we scrutinize ourselves, opportunities, and duties to see what's possible or required. Where something is awry, we fix it, withdraw, or tolerate the dysfunction. Fourth is the diversity of each person's communities and the meanings that bind them.

Meaning in gemeinschaft is uniform: the fans of winning teams exult in the same or similar ways. Not so in societies transformed by reason and efficiency. What is significant for some—a winning team—may be incidental to fans of the loser: responses vary when everything else is the same. What provoked the changes that eventuated in gesellschaft? Plausible candidates include industrialization and education, though all hinge on Descartes's affirmation, "I am, I exist is true necessarily," and its corollaries, that I choose my partners, and with them, our mutual duties. This is freedom of the sort admired by Locke and Mill, liberty anchored in recognition of life-affirming conditions defended (not created) by laws.

Yet we are many, all entitled, and often contentious. Why don't societies teeter on chaos when large numbers of us go our separate ways; are there natural regulators preventing matters from getting out of control? Aristotle said little of law because he supposed that character is the principal social stabilizer.[15] That is mostly true. We could never be vigilant enough if law and the threat of punishment were the only defenses against anarchy; character is the primary control in

MEANING AND NORMATIVITY

all the situations where there are no laws, or none that regulate the ambiguities of daily life. Yet law is no less than a second condition for order in societies where shifting aims and members provoke intra- and intercommunal frictions.

Why do societies settle into stabilizing routines? Could it be that character and conventional laws approximate natural constraints? Both have effects that stabilize social arrangements as they change: character—some degree of judgment, independence, reliability, and purpose—steadies behavior as we experiment; laws equilibrate as they regulate. This balance suggests a degree of convergence between formulaic gemeinschaft and pragmatic gesellschaft: where peace and productivity are life-sustaining attractors for human societies, each qualifies as a locally distorted expression of the natural constraints on social change and instability.

Consider moral identity's distinguishing traits.

Loyalty to core values. People raised in a society locate them-selves—in practice, understanding, feeling, and morals—within its web: the German who can't imagine being French; the Arsenal fan who wouldn't root for Chelsea. Many such values—whether intellectual, emotional, aesthetic, or social—were acquired in childhood. One knows the intensity of these beliefs or persuasions when compromising them would require betraying oneself, yet one who lives in a gemeinschaft society acquires them, because of his or her context, without being responsible for having them. There are similar depths to the commit-ments of gesellschaft, yet its values aren't so firmly rooted. One is aware, if only dimly, that their force derives principally or only from choices and experiences that seem to have justified them.

The meaning or narrative that justifies one's loyalty to a community. Every identity may be explained by the personal story describing one's responses—at home, school, or work—to communal duties: was the response settled and stable from the beginning, or did it evolve? The narrative might be incomplete without deference to the power—God or the Good—responsible for one's submission to community demands. There is also the possibility that loyalty is amply justified by the success of a chosen community, by one's efficacy within it, and by the pleasure of one's relations to its other members.

Norms that regularize life within a community. Communities are unified by norms of several kinds. Some are rules that make us mutually recognizable because we do the same things in the same ways. Others are beliefs about the world and ourselves, including norms that regulate our differences (those governing gender relations, for example). Or the norms are responsible for the purity of our ritualized practices. Wanting such norms is characteristic of gemeinschaft, where experiment is unnecessary because initiative would be disruptive. Having the norms reminds us that personal discipline and social order are conditions for well-being. People of gesellschaft bristle when there is too much law: rules for the sake of etiquette or control, rules for the sake of rules. Yet norms are essential in complex societies where scarce resources and crowding make regulation imperative. The difference here is the source of rules and the domains in which they apply.

Proscriptions that foreclose other choices. Proscriptions are blunt-force norms: they define a community's moral boundaries by specifying the penalties incurred by crossing them. Punishments may be severe: physical torture was once commonplace, though the threat of psychological pain—excommunication, ruptured identity—is also a deterrent.

These have been remarks about moral identity from the perspective of community members. They ignore the perspective of judgments about a community's moral identity: when is a family, friendship, business, or nation judged moral or not? Must the judgment be all-or-nothing—praise or condemnation—or is it often specific to tasks or occasions (good at this, bad at that)? Blanket appraisals are rare because the basis for criticism or praise is usually specific (one of several or many things done well or badly). Yet emphasis on one of them may deservedly unbalance judgments of the whole: their products are beautifully made, though produced by children or slaves working in vile conditions.

It is relatively easy to withhold moral judgments about whole communities when we can distinguish conditions for their specific successes or failures. But that leaves a question this precision averts: when can we plausibly judge the community as a whole morally admirable or deficient? A community's intention is one answer: Is it organized for an aim that's worthy or vicious? Does it behave prudently while caring for its members, or is it so cynical or disorganized that it ignores the well-being of all but its autocratic leaders, or, in extremis, not even them?

Natural Laws

Religious versions of gemeinschaft postulate that societies are located within a divinely ordered cosmos. There are, they aver, laws regulating natural processes and relationships at every scale, whatever their content or complexity. Gesellschaft's fidelity to rational order largely starts and stops at calculations promoting individual or community initiatives. Having little interest in metaphysics, it supposes that laws regulating personal or communal initiatives are pragmatic and conventional, not natural. This would entail that the entire social system of permissions and restraints has no stable basis apart from habit and our willingness to maintain it. It implies that coherence of every sort, like traffic on a heavily traveled road, depends on the stability of a regulatory framework that is only conventional. What is the defense when competition, conflict, and scarce resources threaten to overwhelm that structure? Is there no defense but social habit and goodwill; or could it be that our conventions are sensitive responses to the circumstances in which they apply? There are, for example, several ways to divide traffic so drivers going in opposed direction don't collide. A driver who escapes traffic jams by turning into the empty lanes of on-coming traffic can't plead that driving there was the more efficient way of reaching his destination, because he violates the lifesaving demand for prudence.

Here, as so often, law is the crystallization of practices respectful of life, reciprocity, and our interdependence, all of them scruples required by viable communities. Are the determinable profiles of natural constraints discernible amid the material complexities of our social practices: separate circles of freedom for children and adults, men and women? Would we avoid conflicts by estimating what they may be; or would every putative estimate be dismissed as the idealization or distortion of a conventional value? Can we accurately distinguish the conventional from the natural, or do we err in the other direction by obscuring natural differences when we reify conventional practices?

88 COMMUNITY

Emphasizing freedom of choice, we override traditional constraints, but is that always prudent? Why not go the other way: stop the dispute by identifying domains of constraining natural forms? Both family and friendship, for example, exemplify community and interdependence, each with its cultural variations. Individuals, however stubbornly separate, don't alter the impression that these modes of socialization are founded in the natural vectors of purpose and need.

Regard for natural laws would clarify some disputes by obliging us to distinguish their constraints from the permissions or restrictions favored by current values. But this is contentious, for how are we to discern natural laws with precision when they are obscured by the accidents of contemporary practice? Why suppose that any practice violates a law if we can't specify it by citing examples purged of these overlays? Physics distinguishes laws of motion from force laws having application in particular domains. Sociology is less adept because cultural overlays are conventions disguising underlying constraints. This uncertainty—constricting laws or reckless variability—is consequential for human practice if there are natural laws regulating what we do, and if distorting or ignoring them has effects we rue. Are there systems or societies that struggle for stability and coherence because mistaken assumptions about human behavior are opposed by stubborn natural forms?

Chapter Four

Autonomy

Autonomy—self-sufficiency in judgment and action—is qualified by genetics and socialization. They speak in each of us before circumstances overlay appetite and inclination with roles and duties. Why this qualified reading of Mill's *On Liberty*? Because community is agency's context; we learn and express our freedom in the company of those who share interests that none can satisfy alone.

We proceed in two steps. The first requires choices appropriate to common needs. Give help to get it; know how to satisfy the task at hand, then find capable partners. The other is instruction in moral sensibility; people engaging one another sometimes choose responsibility for their well-being. We evolve as Rousseau and Kant thought we should: to equal emphasis on freedom and fraternity. Yet Locke and Mill extolled the individualism that dominates libertarian social thinking. They affirmed, with Plato and Aristotle, that well-socialized people can be intellectually and morally self-sufficient. This was Luther's posture when he wrote of souls responsible principally to God; so was Descartes's *cogito* self-sufficient: "I am, I exist is necessarily true whenever . . . it is conceived in my mind."[1] "But what then . . . am I? A thing that doubts, understands, affirms, denies, is willing, is unwilling."[2] Mill buttressed their emphasis on autonomy with a curious flaw: "It is, perhaps, hardly necessary to say that this doctrine is meant to apply only to human beings in the maturity of their faculties. We are not speaking of children or of young persons below the age which the law may fix as that of manhood or womanhood . . . Liberty, as a principle, has no application to any state of things anterior to the time when mankind have become capable of being improved by free and equal discussion."[3] Children need education of all sorts—practical, intellectual, moral, and emotional—yet their capacities are commensurate with their deficiencies; they acquire autonomy with the skills learned while thinking, doing, or making in the company of other people. They may also realize that autonomy is marked Peruvian, Chinese, French, or American because skills, tastes, and inhibitions are inflected by an agent's culture.

Mill's three regions of freedom—thought, tastes and pursuits, and the power to combine with others—rightly identify autonomy's principal expressions while distorting its evolution. Freedom of thought and choice emerge in contexts where children have examples, direction, and opportunities to choose and explore. They aren't innate, except to the degree that nervous systems sputter erratically in the absence of nurture and education. This is a measure of a child's education: What choices does it promote? Are imagination and initiative motivated and enabled? Remember a time when it was true to say: before, I couldn't read; now that I can—though only in the language of my culture—I choose my books.

Autonomy is empowered, not drowned, by socialization. Collaboration obscures it if a system's members are perceived as mere functionaries when observed in their roles. That perception disguises what socialization has achieved: that childhood is an apprenticeship in the choices and roles of adulthood. Choice is critical, though paradoxically it's a power acquired by submitting to the disciplines of childhood. Children learn how to behave in situations they haven't chosen; they learn to choose well in situations where options are few and mistakes are avoided because they've acquired habits of judgment. This is autonomy—powers adapted in maturity but acquired in childhood, capacities too often suppressed when formulaic roles and circumstances preclude their use.

Mill was careless: he declared that thought and choice are exempt from material conditions such as socialization because principal thinkers had been emphasizing autonomy since Descartes's "I am, I exist each time I think . . . What am I? A thinking thing."[4] Why is this a sufficient characterization of things that think? Because nothing more is required if, after the first *Meditation*, the isolated thinker doesn't need socializing and can't have it: here I am, thinking of myself, when nothing else exists. Yet the first two *Meditations* are as much theater as analysis; inferring from them to truths about autonomy ignores thought's context: being unschooled and unsocialized deprives it of form and focus. Workmates don't care that others intuit ideas or themselves; they need to know that partners use a common language to speak of accessible means and ends. Collaborations would be less likely to succeed if partners weren't formed in ways making the expectations of others mutually intelligible.

How does autonomy survive socialization? The question is upside-down: autonomy is enabled by one's relations with teachers or partners; learning from them, one goes on to different or harder challenges while working with others. Some capacities for thought or will are likely innate, yet their acquired powers are measured against the challenges in which agents learn to think, explore, and act. Does one have the motivation and skill partners require? Not if they ask me, a cellist, to play a bassoon. Autonomy is conditional but real: lacking the relevant education and skill, I would be incompetent in every context, though I can play with others in situations appropriate to their skills and mine.

Fragility

Socialized learning is fragile because skills and motivation go fallow if teaching situations don't recur: This effect seems odd if we assume, with Descartes's second *Meditation*—that autonomy is a capacity for thinking or acting irrespective of context, but this is not the autonomy of those whose choices were honed when teachers taught them judgment in problematic situations. One imagines the contrary view, that someone knowing no Japanese may learn it by spending whatever time is required to understand one of its books without the help of a teacher. Some linguists may imagine finding their way into a language they can't yet decipher; the rest of us would be stymied. What does this prove? That self-sufficiency is limited: having freedom of choice and action is a power acquired in a context and sustained by practicing its skills in situations similar to those of their learning.

Gemeinschaft supposes that we are loyal to the roles assigned us by God or birth. Gesellschaft observes that our actions are prescribed, principally, by self-interest and imagined benefits; roles chosen at any moment may differ from those pursued when oversight advises that the lights have changed. For if every bond is contingent, we could rethink it and withdraw, ignoring our duties to a system's other members. Loyalty is precarious if we're free to override every commitment by deserting any role. But that isn't the social message we learn, or the freedom acquired with autonomy. Its ambit is narrow: What am I currently doing or responsible for doing? Why did I choose or affirm a role I inherited? Do I know how to satisfy it? How might I do it differently or better? How distasteful or abusive need it be before I withdraw?

Acting as routine prescribes is defeating if stasis is enfeebling; change is desirable if an established routine is less effective than one newly possible. Autonomous agents make that judgment. Their initiatives are the motors of effective change when the choice of disruption or routine is a cogent moral judgment: What is owed the future, how much to the past? Rigor demands that both possibilities—routine and renewal—are acknowledged, though conviction may falter as we lean either way. How do we subordinate appraisal and choice to the imperatives of organizational stability? Balance is elusive. This doesn't imply that established ways are often replaced, only that autonomy is required if one or more of a system's members are to make the judgment that arrangements need to change.

Networks and Other Constraints

We inherit systems and roles that resist change while addressing the world with a question: is there something useful or enticing we could be doing—something just beyond our reach? This is the attitude of people responsible for relationships they choose or affirm, and responsible to a lesser degree for the networks in which they participate. Duties to one's systems are usually known; duties to their networks are often obscure.

Networks of three kinds are apparent: (1) those responsible for providing resources vital to one's vocation (staff, shops, and transport);

AUTONOMY 93

(2) the cluster of systems generated by a personal interest or need (services supporting schools one's children attend); and (3) the networks of one's partners (a spouse's friends). Autonomy—one's power to choose for reasons of one's own—obscures these connections because we imagine arranging social furniture to our taste, and because they seem remote. Why disregard them? Because the Enlightenment—"Man is born free but is everywhere in chains"[5]—declared that we are or can be exempt from the effects of other people and things, and because the Industrial Revolution caused, then purged, some of its corrosive effects on labor. Libertarian Americans are also shaped by the history of the frontier where freedom from one's circumstances seemed merged with freedom to choose: when going West assured that church and state wouldn't control one's life or aims because they were barely a presence, and because personal effort was the principal or only means to survival. Yet the frontier is long closed; most of us live in metropolitan centers where thought, imagination, and action are everywhere limited and directed. Educated and nurtured while formed for conventional tasks, we're shaped by roles we haven't designed and can't alter. Autonomy in them is restricted, principally, to acquiring or applying standardized skills or beliefs while engaging partners who do the same. We learn the techniques and standards of established roles because routinized practice eases communication among cooperating agents; like musicians playing established scores, we play our parts without improvising.

The rigidity of our practices is nevertheless hard to sustain because it's punishing and often ineffective. Working within a format—marriage, for example—makes one's tasks intelligible to partners, until the force of another personality requires other responses. For everything formulaic yields to the realization that its form is provisional. There are, for example, no formulas prescribing the detailed profiles of prospective friends because friendship is testimony to the idiosyncrasies of the people bonding; even vocations are hard to prescribe if schools teach initiative and economies tolerate diversity. Choice and personal development expose the visible differences of taste and feeling that register when we choose our roles and companions. Autonomy looks two ways: to innovations that cohere, over time, in established formats. Cubist

94 COMMUNITY

paintings fill rectangular frames; architects design iconic buildings for sites having specific dimensions.

Yet any role—inherited or chosen, formulaic or improvised—is seen to require autonomy once we distinguish roles from the perspective of agents obliged to learn them and the situations in which they're satisfied. For there is the difference of roles and their duties versus the variable skills and circumstances of a system's members. This is autonomy, the existential variable in social practice. Accepting a role, one accepts its duties; enacting the role is the additional task of bending it to the shape of one's abilities. Doing this successfully is a matter of skill, imagination, and will. Robots may have no margin for variability, but people do. Variations, like diner coffee, are usually accepted without comment if they fall within an expected range. Workers are usually content if attention isn't called to whatever is distinctive in their efforts, though a distinguishing edge is often the effect of conscious effort. Satisfying many roles exhausts the energy and attention of most agents. Others, less compliant, resist arbitrary limits and routines: they garden as others do, but see the difference they make. Significant variation comes mostly from those with viable aims, allies, and means. But they, too, struggle because social systems don't yield if routines produce reliable effects: "better the devil you know . . ." infuses rhythms wherever people know what to do because they're reproved for doing otherwise.

Contextual expressions of idiosyncrasy and skill are two of autonomy's markers but not usually the ones emphasized when thinking of liberty. Those of us having choices express ourselves freely in thought, movement, or action; we aren't free to think of everything or free to do or go anywhere, but we are free to choose within each of these spheres from an array of possibilities made visible by interest, education, or opportunity: tennis or golf, music or dance. Socialization's role is different in these contexts: established roles can be satisfied in ways that make allowances for individual skills; here the determinants are personal taste, talent, or desire. Freedom in the first case is the latitude that others show us as we satisfy a role or duty; here freedom is an expression of sensibility. What do you like? Do we have styles or vocations that please you? If, yes, enjoy those on hand; if not, amend what's available, or experiment with something new. It's a contingency that we have these freedoms, and politics, power, or luck—not only socialization—that prevents others from having them.

Obstacles

Is duty an obstacle to autonomy, or is autonomy channeled by duty? Duty is a social demand: act as you said or implied you would. The intention it expresses couples to a partner's expectation that the duty will be fulfilled. This complementarity may be conscious ("I promise . . .") or repetition in a practice creates expectations in both partners. Singing duets, knowing where we are in the score, you know what to expect of me, and I of you. Duty is a social precipitate, the moral and psychological commitment to a relationship, the promise to act as a role requires if a collaboration is to have its intended aim. It deters either of us from walking away before the song is done. Autonomy is qualified by duty when choice and action are subordinate to systems and roles one has inherited, joined, or created. This is the schizoid posture of nodes: they're obliged to satisfy the ensemble of roles they have chosen or inherited and affirmed. You didn't have to choose this role, but you did, so act as your partners expect.

Is either—duty or freedom—subordinate to the other or do agents live perpetually in the tension of having to favor one or the other? Resolution is obscured by the idea of freedom vaunted in Mill's *On Liberty*. The freedom it describes is conditioned in two ways: by Mill's no-harm principle (do nothing that would damage others), and by duties acquired when uniting with others for common or complementary aims. Agreeing to join others in pursuit of an aim or defense of an interest, one is duty-bound to see the effort through to its conclusion (the duties having been agreed in contracts that are written, oral, or tacit). Yet autonomy is allegedly inalienable, while contracts are instruments presupposing one's freedom to affirm or deny their terms. Duties acquired contractually are transitory; they lapse after a specified outcome or date. A contract is violated if one ignores duties it stipulates, but there is a remedy, Mill implies: pay limited costs to the wounded party because duties are alienable as autonomy is not.

Mill's idea of freedom locates us near the last pages of Plato's *Republic*, where his version of democracy—narcissism intensified by personal freedom—risks anarchy. Philosopher kings could be trusted with autonomy in the performance of executive tasks because their choices would be constrained by their knowledge of Forms illumined by the Good. Everyone else would have acquired duties while learning fidelity to specific roles: guardian or artisan. Yet no one in Plato's ideal state would have unconditional autonomy, because no one would be trusted to make decisions founded only on his or her taste, discretion, or judgment. Every role would be contextualized: by routine, discipline, or illumination. Mill disagreed: any role requires agents who qualify for it because information, discipline, and judgment enable them to assume it without requiring the oversight of others or a context where a deus ex machina (soul and conscience, or the light of the Good) precludes bad choices. Duty requires fidelity to one's roles because of loyalty to one's systems and their other members. Yet these extremes—Plato and Mill—ambiguate autonomy's relation to duty. Nodes choose both their roles and the time and effort devoted to each.

Is there an acceptable balance of harms: systems sabotaged by their members versus members frustrated by their duties? It seems to libertarians that Hume relieved us of guilt by arguing that there is no natural normativity. Where duty and morality are conventional—because justified by inclinations and feelings only—no breach of duty is more than a psychological or conventional disappointment, a disruption in the rhythms of personal expectation or the conventions of social life. Productive communities—families, schools, businesses, and governments—are merely the constricted milieus in which autonomous agents suppress their natural autonomy: we choose partners and vocations promising some degree of satisfaction and material comfort, though choices and duties are contingencies. Agents can change their minds, *ought* isn't derivable from *is*. We cite "duties" to stabilize profitable relationships, though harm to oneself or others is the whole cost of violating them. Others may be annoyed, but let them collect damages; they, too, are free to choose trajectories that suit them.

Hume had a Cartesian standard for confirming the absence of natural normativity: argument would have to prove that negating the idea of something allegedly necessary is a contradiction. But no one believes that abandoning one's children is contradictory, merely that doing it violates the duty of care. Yet the issue isn't resolved. Illness may explain a caretaker's neglect, but that would extenuate duty's application, not the duty itself; it may be necessary in its context. For it's true generally that normativities in human social domains are material and contextual; their negations are rarely or never contradictions. But no human survives without food, clothing, and sleep: is that a necessary truth? Call it a *parochial necessity*: one applying to the humans of our world. One may imagine creatures like us in every way except that a different physiology enables them to live without our needs. Resources, including the help of other people, are, nevertheless, material necessities in our world: we can't live without them.

What is freedom's value if agents having it can't override relationships they've chosen or inherited and affirmed? My neighbor is elderly and feeble. She cared for herself until recently but can't anymore. Do I have the duty of care? It isn't the duty I would have to my mother, wife, or daughter, but we have been mutually helpful for years. I could turn away but won't. Community is social glue; freedom in this situation is the duty of foresight and care: an obligation established by proximity, custom, and need. Others can decide what to call it—vanity or a conceit—though notice that Hume and the Mill of *On Liberty* have already impoverished conversations in which *natural normativity* is a phrase without sense. Is convention the only defense against the risk that all may freely ignore situations having any degree of moral weight? No, there is a web of laws, expectations, and punishments intrinsic to the fabric of social relations. Some constituents—traffic laws—are conventional; duties to one's partners and systems are natural in the respect that duties in core communities and utilities are the consequence of our interdependencies: unable to satisfy all our needs alone, we are bound to our partners. Natural normativity in practical life is an array of reciprocities: each person bound to others because none is altogether self-reliant and because we freely commit ourselves to reciprocities in which we give help or the promise of it to get help.

These are the nuts and bolts of social life, but *Utilitarianism* cut through this clutter, with a clarity recorded in the *Dedication* to *On Liberty*: "To the beloved and deplored memory of her who was the inspirer, and in part the author of all that is best in my writings—the friend and wife whose exalted sense of truth and right was my strongest incitement, and whose approbation was my chief reward—I dedicate this volume. Like all that I have written for many years, it belongs as much to her as to me."[6] Interdependence has effects on the psychology and practices of a society's collaborating members: expectation, gratitude, and disappointment are its reliable sentiments. Guilt is another: the punishments for breaking traffic laws are fines, though the punishment for injuring faultless pedestrians is guilt. Are guilt's expressions more variable than this implies: could one feel guilty rather than embarrassed about using the wrong fork or because dressed inappropriately at a funeral? Perhaps, though only if humiliated when challenged for choices one knew to be inappropriate. Guilt, like shame, is a deep measure of one's vulnerability to the perceptions of others in a social world where autonomy is steeply qualified.

Rules constrain the rhythms of practical experience; the laws expressing such rules transform expectations into demands. But the laws are late additions to relationships they constrain. Someone wanting to understand the origins of duty emphasizes the textures of practical life, their reciprocities and expectations, not laws.

Communal Authority

Roles are assigned, work is appraised; autonomy jostles with communal authority. But authority is unexplained if communities are nothing other than assemblies of people bound by shared interests, feelings, and aims. How do we come to be controlled by systems that are collections of ourselves? Some reasons invoke the organizational or legislative authority of sovereign states, but what we construe as authority is often the effect of custom, bureaucracy, or inertia. How, for example, does one challenge communities-of-meaning that deny positions of authority to half their congregants? Is there a posture that legitimizes a change in the view of the community challenged, or is there no legitimizing posture, so opposition reduces to defiance and struggle?

Communities-of-interest deserve challenges to their authority if they cripple the utility for which they're responsible or if one of their accessory functions (budget, for example) is mishandled: clients stop buying or paying; participants quit. Communities-of-meaning are less effective when staring down their critics because there is little leverage for challenging whatever they do internally, short of criminality. An organization can ignore critics; an association may hardly notice when they drift away. What authority does meaning—emotion or interpretation—bestow? Only, though sufficiently, the power of massed accord; the authority to proceed or practice as a community is just the unanimity of a community's members (including a majority's deference to the will of a minority). But friends fall out, marriages fail; discipline fails because unanimity founders.

Does a community-of-meaning have this authority if accord is the effect of coercion or mute custom? Many communities have coercive power over their paralyzed members; but power is a force, not the authority that bestows a right, in this case the membership's right to organize and sustain group identity. Is there authority in the corporate entity—the community—or only in the collectivity of its membership.? Is marriage the coupling of separate people, or both of them plus "the couple" created by their marriage?

Socialized autonomy implies deference to communities one has voluntarily joined or affirmed when inherited. Yet socialization doesn't entail an obligation in all circumstances to the supererogatory interest of the marriage or friendship. When is divorce an option? Socialization makes us restrained: people are usually willing to suffer a degree of stress before separating themselves from an affiliation they once chose. They're slow to act, especially as they calculate the effects on other members or accept a diminished idea of themselves.

This is autonomy's existential expression: each participant's raw power to say yes or no; I want it or I don't. Every voluntary adult relationship is grounded, this implies, in the willing participation of its members. Socialization's claim stops short of communal ownership; determined to separate myself from a community of either sort—interest or meaning—I resign. This is the power cosmetically described as a natural right, but that is an obscure disguise for autonomy swathed in the power of will. One declines subordination to the community in which one participated, the system with which one identified, acknowledging the distress of those remaining and one's pain.

Why are will, consent, and autonomy freedom's moral foundation? Because there is, in gesellschaft, no ulterior ground from which to judge when socialization is breached. Gemeinschaft's prescription—no divorce—would have stopped the slide before it could be resolved by personal choice. Talk of gesellschaft's deference to autonomy is partly cosmetic. The ideas to which it appeals—as in Mill's *On Liberty*—are alien to circumstances where choice is suppressed by one's vulnerability to conditions that are social, political, economic, or psychological. There, as in despotic versions of gemeinschaft, few choices exist.

Justice

Justice that's distributive or procedural requires that everyone be given his or her due. Contention begins as we're specific about the implications of "one's due." Is it procedural only—subject to the same laws applied in the same ways—or substantive, too, because subject to costs and benefits common to all, or because costs and benefits are rightly proportionate to one's merits or attributes (young or old, male or female)? Does the domain of recipients start and stop with a distribution to individual persons or should it include costs or benefits to their families, businesses, and towns? Our individualist convictions are dogmatic, plain, and reinforced by the United States Supreme Court's ruling in *Citizens United v. Federal Election Commission*:[7] rights and duties appropriate to individual citizens do not apply to their organizations because those are aggregates: collections of individuals distinguished by a title. One may have duties to individuals, but not, this ruling would imply, to their relationships: families, friendships, tribes, or states.

The justification for *Citizens United* is a suppressed quarrel about relations and their products. Do relations reduce to conjunction? Are relationships no more than individuals collected under a name? Or do relations (especially causal reciprocities) create entities (relationships, systems) that are distinguishable but not separable from their members? The issue is contested, though some examples fall unassailably to a side: the solar system is more than an aggregate. Its stability, dynamics, and predictability are secured because causal reciprocity—in the form of gravity—regulates the relations of its parts. So, too, is friendship the entity created when reciprocities bind the friends. Each acknowledges, however implicitly, that he or she has duties to their system and to one another. Why this doubled referent: separate duties satisfied by the same action? Because mutuality has created the relationship on which friends depend for some degree of their well-being. Why emphasize this categorial difference? Because logical atomism and individualism ignore the interpersonal weave of reciprocities constitutive of social systems, and the ramified, often hierarchical contexts where intellectual, moral, and practical bonds are acquired and exercised. Atomists simplify social life by distorting it: they abstract individuals from circumstances where they acquire autonomy, links, and responsibilities. What does this imply about our duties to relationships we condemn, including pernicious systems willingly joined? Responsibility to them is implied, though one may have an overriding duty to the sovereign that bans them.

Universalizing ideas of justice require equal rights and equal opportunities for all, conditions that aren't satisfied if individuals can't depend on the satisfaction of duties that others—individuals or systems—have to them. But there is this complement: Is it just that individuals are casual or reckless when failing to satisfy their duties to the social systems to and for which they're responsible? Does the converse also apply: that systems should avoid responsibility for their duties by pretending that they are, after all, merely names—General Motors, the *New York Times*—used as labels for collections of people who sometimes collaborate? Let recognition go both ways: to individuals responsible for duties incurred when systems are chosen or affirmed when inherited; and to communities or utilities responsible for their effects on members, other systems, the environment, and bystanders.

Citizens United is shallow ontology. Its fault is the ungrounded assumption that individuals, but not systems of any size or structure, have identity, structural integrity, or interests. But what shall count as individuals? Descartes made that easy by reducing all reality to individual consciousness, though physics accomplished a parallel feat by affirming that matter is a complex of particles. Hence the conundrum that gesellschaft's analytic style has encouraged an individualism for which there is no stopping point short of minds, molecules, atoms, or their constituents. Everything larger on any scale is, on this view, an aggregate having no essential integrity. This is troubling if we suppose that justice requires a fair distribution of available rights, benefits, or resources to persons and communities, when justice for quarks seems a category mistake. For there is no ontological justification for stopping the reduction of aggregates anywhere short of foundational particles, unless we grant the reality and efficacy of relations—the generative effects of efficient and formal causes—hence, the emergent orders of molecules, cells, bodies, tribes, and states.

Gesellschaft's sponsors aren't usually sensitive to these ontological concerns. They stop the ontological regress at the scale of humans out of regard for Descartes, Mill, and thought's autonomy; let each person choose his or her aims when the no-harm principle constrains their choices. All would be well if aggregates were orderly and productive, though the tasks of higher-order systems—families, schools, and businesses—couldn't be performed if spatial-temporal relations were their only bonds. The cure is twofold: recognize that causal relations are responsible for generating stable, productive systems; and that their aims and efficacy are the work of their collaborating members. Let these agents acknowledge that they straddle two orders: separate bodies and the social systems formed by their reciprocal causal relations. Dynamic complexity—causality and energy exchange—enables people and their systems to do what their least parts couldn't do alone. Justice is shortchanged when the Supreme Court affirms that individuality and autonomy are the only things of worth. We distribute rights, goods, and duties to complex entities: people and their communities.

Gesellschaft's respect for individual freedom is too simple; we fled enthusiastically from holist autocracy without considering that autonomy is a power conditioned by interdependence. Ideas of duty, togetherness, and justice are richer than it implies; we're no longer

AUTONOMY 103

surprised that collaboration is the condition for achievements in art, science, and practical life. There would be few or none if individuals or crowds were left to produce them alone.

Free Will

Need would likely guarantee the formation of communities-of-interest and -meaning if there were no free will. But sometimes, when unfamiliar or problematic circumstances defeat habit and instinct, will and imagination are essential to choice and well-being. We have richer choices than rabbits or squirrels, though no more freedom than theirs if we lack free will. Hard determinism—the notion that everything has material antecedents sufficient to determine its existence, character, and its every next action or state—reduces us to mechanical toys pushed and pulled by conditions that include our programmed internal states. Kant supposed that we have free will: the noumenal mind chooses "spontaneously" while logically prior to and ontologically distinct from the experiences it schematizes.[8] Yet this is the implausible claim of his psychic mechanics: mind, like God, is independent of, and logically prior to the experiences it creates. Revert to hard determinism, and we concede that our seeming self-control is just the wake of our antecedents. The alleged tension between self and society is an illusion if this is true: everything swims in a sea of multiply linked causes; no intervention alters to any degree the direction of a tide that sweeps through everything and everybody. Communities emerge because their members converge mechanically, not because they choose their partners and aims.

It would be incidental in the vast scale of things had nature given us the false sense of having choices exempting us to a small degree from the effects of our antecedents. But it is consequential for self-understanding that hard determinism ignores a determinist alternative with six parts.

First is the uncertainty, sometimes the confusion that comes with situations that are odd, different from others one has known, or merely different in provocative ways. We stop to consider what to do, because there may not be obvious or favorable ways to respond.

104 COMMUNITY

Protons are likely indifferent to their histories, though determined by them. What will they do? Where will they go next? Do they scatter or follow long-established trajectories? That depends on what happens nearby, not only on where they've been. It's plausible that the behavior of each, like the murmuration of individual birds, is wholly predictable given comprehensive information about them. Yet human agents add powers they lack: namely, inhibition and deliberation. We resist impulses that would have us respond recklessly because we're not sure what to do. Taking time to acquire information about our circumstances and options, we act in ways that are free in the same respect that our actions are calculated and chosen.

Third is this altered view of the events provoking us: delay enables deliberation. We consider alternative responses to a provoking cause: which action or judgment would be appropriate to our circumstances, interests, or values? Rather than trace every response to the causal lineage initiated at the beginning of time, we cite a current provocation: yesterday's earthquake, not something in our past, which requires a response. Hard determinists—always assuming that deliberation is invariably loaded with the past—cite three views of predestination: (1) the idea that every agent embodies within itself causes and a causal history sufficient to determine its every next action; (2) the view that agents coalesce when their independent development has made them compatible; and (3) Leibniz's claim that every coupling is predestined from the time of the world's creation because the character of each depends to some degree on the character of everything else. Options 1 and 3 aver that Jack and Jill were fated to meet; there was nothing uncertain about the outcome as they tested one another. But option 2 implies that their meeting was accidental not fated: they were preformed in complementary ways, but with no intimation that their meeting would be other than accidental. Hard determinists rely on options 1 and 3. Individuals advance blindly, whatever their illusions, for reasons—causes—that prefigure all they can do or be (Jack would meet and bond to a woman like Jill, or this very Jill, whatever his intentions); or outcomes are assured because of the deep causal weave locating every individual in mutually determining relations to every other, near or far.

Yet Jack and Jill don't spontaneously coalesce; their courtship is an experiment. They test one another before each has learned to accommodate the other; their friendship is an outcome, not an effect preformed. This persuasion is challenged by a narrative that hard determinists can't defend. For no evidence confirms either idea of predestination: 1 or 3. Individuals surprised by unforeseen situations hesitate because they don't know what to do; foundering in Leibnizian complexities, they withdraw to evaluate and choose. Is every individual trajectory prefigured: no accidents, encounters, discoveries, or reflections divert us from a path decided at the beginning of time? Is everything connected, its character determined to some degree by everything else? Not when every name, number, and address in a telephone directory is undetermined by its relations to those before or after it.

Last is the action chosen: agents launch themselves into the near world in ways determined by judgments that couldn't have been predicted by an observing god without details of several kinds: an inventory continuously updated with information about their interactions in the near world; the shifting state of their inclinations and vulnerabilities; and the changing priorities or values affected by new information, altered beliefs, and labile emotions. This is information pertinent to current circumstances, information that isn't archived or prefigured.

Now we repeat these steps while imagining that something surprising has happened or merely that there are several possible responses, each justifiable if information, values, and interests are weighed differently. There are four phases as we respond to problematic situations: First is inhibition. Often affected by other things, we've acquired defenses that include a resistant outer surface and the power of inhibiting habitual or impulsive responses. Some defenses may have ancient antecedents; many or most others are learned in situations experienced as we age. Second is deliberation, a power for assessing our circumstances before acting. Established values and habits prepare us for current circumstances, though many situations have aspects that give us pause. Needing information, we're careful observers; otherwise imagination, enhanced by extrapolation or analogy, designs possible responses. Third is the choice of an appropriate response. We may decide to do nothing; though each plan of action has three parts: a map of the circumstances likely to be encountered, the steps to be taken, and (less explicitly) fallback responses to frustration or resistance. Fourth is an action that tests the ambient world. These four—from inhibition through deliberation to action—are the responses of an agent controlling (to some degree) a situation and itself in circumstances that are problematic because he or she has no prepared response.

The causal tide diverges ever so slightly when choice resolves an uncertainty. Yet hard determinists regard this sequence as a charade; we take appearances—including the illusion of deliberation and our apparent liberty to intervene—as nearly irrefutable evidence of will's freedom, though Descartes's remarks about dreams should have taught us otherwise. They dispute the possibility of free will because of the more radical surmise that no choice is exempt from the full weight of its causal history. A powerful god would foresee every effect prefigured since the beginning of time. These determinists locate our apparent but bogus moments of decision within sequences like those of motion-picture reels, every choice and action the effect of frames sequenced to evoke it. Yet this interpretation, rigidity apart, makes dubious assumptions. Memory, for example, is often experimental in circumstances where it is more like imagination than an archive. Addressing situations for which we have no established response, we consider remembered options while figuring how they're to be modified or ignored, given our circumstances, values, and aims. Imagine tourists confounded when they set out to explore nearby streets. This is Venice, where the local postman is faultless in his neighborhood but unable to find his way nearby. How long before experience enables these visitors to go from their hotel to breakfast without getting lost? Or they're lost each time because always disoriented. Don't we often reflect, imagine, and experiment because we're unprepared?

Free will is a misnomer: my proposal doesn't allege that any choice lacks conditions sufficient to determine both that it is and what it is; events are caused because all are the effects of energy exchange or its inhibition (and because nothing comes to be from nothing). Will isn't unconditioned; it isn't free. Choices are always directed by beliefs or values that evolve as we appraise successive actions—tests—and their effects.

AUTONOMY 107

But soft determinism construes the four phases above as a sequence that originates within agents detached from their circumstances to the degree that their responses are provoked by current circumstances, not by episodes in ancient history. Jack and Jill's meeting is an accident, for which neither is prepared. Lacking information sufficient to make prudent choices, they experiment to learn more. A cosmic intelligence, integrating denumerably infinite detail, might have been able to imagine their resolution without being able to deduce it from its antecedents. This is choice taking directions that quashes ancient biases by correcting them.

Is free will incidental to community formation because affiliation happens irrespective of these conceptual disputes? Purpose, control, and morale make the issue cogent if hard determinists imply that we could reasonably hunker in place waiting for the wind that alternately collects or disperses us. The principle they affirm—sufficient reason—holds that every action has causes sufficient to determine its existence and character. But that doesn't entail that all of an action's causes fall within an actor's history; its principal cause may be the contemporary state of affairs provoking it, not any feature of his or her past.

Hard determinists want to turn our attention 180 degrees away from a future we may accommodate to a past we can never alter. Argument doesn't convince them because their determinism, like theology, is unfalsifiable; one can always allege that an effect has hidden, but unknown causes. Is there evidence that every choice and action is a further plank in a succession whose conditions lie in the past, or is choice deferred until the evidence of an unfamiliar situation—its risk or opportunity—is weighed against information, aims, and values?

"To thine own self be true"

What we call autonomy is often willing deference to established roles and relations: we choose to do as they require. Autonomy doesn't survive without the well-being nourished and stabilized by interdependence; it can't thrive without subordination to systems responsible for our well-being. This is a dilemma with seven viable solutions:

How are community and autonomy mutually affecting? Community and autonomy seem opposed, given freedom's two slogans: *freedom to* and *freedom from*. Freedom from is exemption from any role or duty that isn't chosen or affirmed when inherited; freedom to is the power to go one's way, whatever the disruption to others. A flag from the American Revolution features a coiled snake and the phrase "Don't tread on me": it implies the resistance evoked when Descartes argued that any belief or edict is dubitable if its negation is not a contradiction. Revolutions start in some version of Cartesian autonomy: I am, I exist as a thinking being, one able to doubt, deny, and refuse.[9] Freedom from is the power to extract oneself from a situation or community perceived as inimical or merely intolerable. It provoked Rousseau's observation that "Man is born free but is everywhere in chains." That stroke drew all the plausibility from both monarchies and the religions claiming God as source of their earthly authority.

Every affiliation restricts freedom of both sorts. It limits freedom from because commitment implies a duty to the relationship chosen. Communities shrink the range of activities appropriate to members acting in their name; loyalty to them opposes the aim of liberating oneself from a system's duties. Commitment has a deflating effect on a member's freedom to act as he or she chooses: systems and their roles make specific demands while discouraging or prohibiting random impulses. Do this or do that, but nothing that would embarrass or deter us.

There is also this complementary question, one having no universal solution: What shall I do with my freedom to choose—what shall I do or be? Community is vital to the implied solution if we suppose that interdependence is an essential condition for well-being. Which skills shall I have, where and with whom might I use them? which actions of mine would help to turn utilitarian relations into those of fellowship? Will I still take pleasure in choices made long ago, choices I can't easily renounce, when it's too late for others? Every privileged lifetime in our post-Cartesian world is an answer to this challenge: Which choices were empowered by our freedom to choose? Which of them flourished or survived when escape would have been expensive for others or oneself?

Is duty to oneself separable from duties to one's social systems, partners, and other people? Duties to others are often clear; powerful others may insist that they be satisfied. Yet self-regard may be the fulcrum in every sensibility for *ought*'s derivation from *is*: finding value in myself, I may deem my interests and needs more exigent than many or all others. That isn't the final word for parents, friends, soldiers, and teammates who regularly make contrary choices. Egoism's defenders may reply that altruism has private rewards—the good feelings that come with conscious self-sacrifice—though the soldier falling on a grenade to save a platoon acts impulsively without feeling good about it.

We try to avert these standoffs by reducing costs on both sides. But, revealingly, the absence of a decisive principle—lean one way or the other—implies recognition that individual interests may counterbalance duties to others. This is the cultural bias of a society that emphasizes individual prerogatives; other societies, with a stronger commitment to social coherence, would likely emphasize the priority of duties to one's systems. Yet they, too, would acknowledge the dilemma of people having multiple duties and no time, energy, or resources for satisfying all of them. The working parent can't be in two places at once, hence recognition that regard for an agent's powers and well-being mitigates his or her obligations. One imagines social policies that reduce these conflicts with judicious interventions: day care or working from home.

Do we rightly consider withdrawing from relationships and their duties because we're exhausted by pursuing tasks in muddled or spartan crcumstances? There is a discernible difference between these perspectives: my systems require more than I can give or do versus circumstances that are averse to any plan of mine. Could either perception have been foreseen before responsibilities were acquired? People who accept their roles are presumed to have considered their viability, though one could be pardoned for missing the likely obstacles. Agents and their systems often respond with a practical solution—they avert disappointment by lowering expectations: do what you can.

Can we abandon roles and their systems without damaging those whose duties and expectations require our reliable participation? The fantasy of shucking one's duties is likely familiar to everyone who sticks to a task for a salary or until the obligation expires. But late adolescence—the space between childhood and marriage or a serious job—is perhaps the last moment when responsibility is lightly worn. Most everyone else is embedded in layers of overlapping utilities or communities, and their roles and duties. Systems sputter when reciprocities fail; role-players can't walk away from all of them without hindering worthy projects, confounding other members, or diminishing themselves. Yet we do give notice, leave, and start again with other people in the same or other roles. How is this justified? Often it isn't. Or we explain: this isn't working for me or others; let me try again, elsewhere. This is understood and often excused in cultures that measure loyalty to systems against psychological and material costs to their members.

Can one resign from successive communities without being perceived as unreliable or disloyal? People who doubt a role's viability may have confirming evidence, but that point of view may be incidental to partners who favor the system's aim, other members, their tasks or benefits. Seeing the problem from a distance, they accept that a role and its occupant may not mesh. Yet what's to be done if one's autonomy is sensible to the degree that it's violable in any role or situation? Find work as a shepherd, mail carrier, or any vocation that is less exposed to others' expectations.

Does one willingly declare that personal identity is distinguishable from one's roles? People often separate themselves in reflection from the roles for which they're known; the identity they affirm is a power for acting, not always a particular way of acting. It may be latent or suppressed, a power wanting release in circumstances adverse to its expression: no education, no tools or companions. Is there an effective way to close the gap between the two ideas of self when duties to one's family, business, or state seem so worthy that one satisfies them while suffocating oneself?

People who suffer this trap may choose it when making prudent choices or accepting the alternatives at hand. Unable to save themselves, they imagine saving partners, children, or their principles. But is there a perception of the freedom one has lost when submitting to duties and circumstances one doesn't control? And, if so, what does one do when there are no levers with which to recover or save lost hope? This was life for almost everyone in the West before the Enlightenment and the Industrial Revolution; it is still the fate of most people. There may be consolation in religious communities where the idea of an afterlife appeases disappointment in this one. It is a principal reason for the devotion to local communities: there, at least, one has dignity, fellowship, and mutual understanding.

Does autonomy survive when its excesses are reduced? Rotterdam is dismantling a bridge so a billionaire's new yacht can pass from the boatyard to the sea, though a simpler solution is easily imagined. Need's authentic expressions—those appropriate to individual wants, circumstances, and the interests of others—require that we choose ends whose means are proportionate to the worth and scale of our aims and powers, the burdens inherited by others, their dignity and ours.

Would it have been better for us if duty to oneself had never been imagined? For how could the obligation be satisfied if autonomy is a conceit for everyone immured in mutual dependence without adequate resources? Yet people devoted to a vocation—artists, entrepreneurs, inventors—exhibit their autonomy. Anyone else? Yes, the aunts and grandmothers who devote themselves to caring for others, while revered by their extended families. True to themselves, true to others, they prove that detachment was not freedom's only strategy; they confirm that a vein of autonomy intensifies when devoted to the sociality in which it emerged.

Irresolution

Freedom from and freedom to are cherished ideals. The self-sufficiency they require evokes Locke's 1690 fantasy: "When all the world was America,"[10] a trackless wilderness so large that all could establish self-sufficient homesteads, leagues from neighbors. But this is an idle dream when autonomy is socialized; we acquire fellow feeling, language, practical and cultural skills, then adult vocations in the company of teachers, partners, and communities. Where freedom from all of them would be a misfortune, freedom to is the power to leverage personal talents and cultural skills in the ways and domains of one's society. That balance is hard to strike. Many societies use their members carelessly, without regard for their talents or autonomy. One must be privileged or lucky to avoid lures that stultify rather than liberate, though some people do. Socialized like everyone else, they discover an inclination or talent, a nurturing context—a city, family, business, or school—then a space where acquired skills are perfected. That could be a vocation of many sorts—parent, entrepreneur, or friend—where each exploits his or her autonomy in ways that are personally gratifying and consequential for others. Many people miss this chance; autonomy drowns in the instrumental relations where it emerged.

Chapter Five

Cooperation and Conflict

Interdependence requires working together in ways appropriate to an aim. We collaborate because complex tasks require different skills, or we share our burdens, though our different aims, means, and responsibilities complicate a fair distribution of responsibilities. These details are managed in gemeinschaft societies, because their social designs distribute duties as though they were natural to the people chosen. Competition provokes jostling and disruption in those of gesellschaft because initiatives, tasks, and plans are expedients tested for their resilience, not always because they're appropriate to the people assigned them. This chapter emphasizes issues provoked when burdens are crudely distributed among a community's members; a complementary concern is the way that cooperation and conflict qualify communal relations. (Why is Kentucky's relative share of the national budget so much greater than that of its neighbor, Illinois? Because rich states agree that national standards of well-being should be regularized, and because the Senate minority leader is elected from Kentucky.) They can often be considered without reference to the microrelations of a community's members or its relations—cooperative or competitive—with other communities.

Cooperation

Mutual alignment is a condition for community formation, an effect promoted by rule-governed practices: tennis players cooperate because

113

their game requires it. Social life's procedures aren't always so plain: there are few rules for navigating contentious aims or points of view. Accommodation requires tolerance and compromise or threats and fear. Gesellschaft's members resist intimidation. They concede that others are entitled to act as their roles or interests require, given respect for the no-harm principle or one of equal generality; they expect to encounter aims and views different from their own. People of gemeinschaft may be less resilient because reliable expectations and the security of their roles are principal virtues of their disciplinary space. Competition—challenge—is abrasive: they shouldn't have to defend roles and prerogatives in a society having the holist design they defend.

Cooperation among a System's Members

Cooperation is the result of mutual discovery: what does each of us want, how do we get it; can we satisfy ourselves without thwarting one another? It begins with an informal, barely articulate negotiation: What are your aims? Here are mine. It evolves to considerations of means and responsibilities. This pattern is common to systems forming and to those with roles to fill when established. Yet *cooperation* is vague: it signifies reciprocity when working for an agreed aim, though partners accept inequitable terms when benefits received are better than none or because a coercive system forces acquiescence.

An emphasis on roles and their complementarity is, however, misleading if cooperation is construed in the terms of machines and their replaceable parts. Utilitarian systems require that a role's candidates have skills complementary to those of possible partners, yet people prepared for the same or complementary roles approach them with varying skills and sensibilities. They may converge as partners when engaged by a task, but their respective styles and assumptions may distort their mutual accommodation: not every catcher likes playing with a knuckle-ball pitcher.

Stability and coherence are the effects of cooperation but also its conditions. People accept roles in systems perceived as coherent and stable; dissenters would likely leave or never join. The coherence of a functioning system—a utility or community-of-meaning—is evidence

COOPERATION AND CONFLICT 115

that partners are well matched or viable because mutually tolerant. Yet stability is also a sign that partners know their system's aims and roles, and that each willingly satisfies the other's expectations: they agree about its utility; they like or respect one another.

Community stabilization has several phases. Formation is first: organizations have greater stability when they satisfy a fundamental interest or need. The enthusiasms sustaining associations are vulnerable to time, distractions, or discord. Religious communities endure, fan clubs dissolve. Standardizing the expectations and interactions of role-players is second. Parishioners going from Rome to El Salvador may be surprised by their differences, though ritual practices are stable in both. Testing the receptivity of local society is third: tolerance varies with culture. Communities acceptable in one may be resisted in others.

Cooperation within communities is sometimes sealed when members believe that reality is infused by the dominating spirit of God or the Good: we cooperate as if ascended to Hegel's Absolute. Every member, were this so, would have the same or similar beliefs because their shared resonant ground would establish uniformity in thought, feeling, and intention. We blame ourselves when hopes of transcendence fail; or, given gesellschaft's pragmatic view of affiliation and its emphasis on incentive, we negotiate the practical advantages cooperation achieves. That emphasis leaves many people feeling dissatisfied; they would rather find themselves within a comprehensive cosmic or social order where gemeinschaft's limits and fixed places imply safety. Gesellschaft is uneven by comparison; we scramble to assemble relationships adequate to our needs because we're taught that personal initiative is all the power we have, though enough to guarantee well-being. We're anxious because we're rarely self-sufficient.

Communities seem a better way, but how are they to be organized and led if this is gesellschaft, where each of us insists on the right to make decisions. Why entrust absolutist authority to any person when judgment is so often reckless or poor? Why not trust power in those who rely on traditional solutions for everyday issues? Some problems are the effects of friction. Gemeinschaft intervenes by forcibly suppressing differences. Made in God's image or discovering our identity as workers, men, or women, we are as one; different talents and roles

116   COMMUNITY

seem incidental when we discern our essential identity within the whole. Gesellschaft assumes that differences are real and useful when exploited by utilities that submit to stabilizing rules or laws. Its values are pragmatic: acquire the skills and inclinations appropriate to roles we choose or inherit; understand that cooperation is the condition for living in societies where competition is a cost because opportunity and initiative are premier values while resources are scarce. We're defended by the community-of-accord that encourages initiatives while excusing our impulses, though it requires that agents navigate their spaces prudently. Knowing that competition may be fierce, we acknowledge that success from one perspective may be failure from another.

These are two views of cooperation. One is the idea that we rediscover our spiritual identity, hence the idyllic community—the Eden—from which we seem exiled. The other evokes the negotiations of agents whose interests or needs converge on plans and actions making them mutually useful. Acknowledge our interdependence, while satisfying Kant's demand that other rational beings be regarded as ends, not only as means. For the essence of others is identical with one's own: they, too, are practical beings, potential partners whose interests are sometimes complementary to ours. This is the prudence of agents needing the support of others while pursuing their separate aims. Cooperation is willing submission to the reality of our interdependence.

Gemeinschaft and gesellschaft are rightly perceived as contraries, but an additional variable is critical to both: each is normative. Both make demands that are moral in that they concern the well-being of all humanity or, less ambitiously, all of a community's members. There is evidence of their normativity when people feel guilty for failing to participate in core systems or for failing to act as their roles require. Why feel guilty? Because the combination of a role, one's commitment to its system, and the expectations of partners establish a duty fulfilled by satisfying the role. We meet this standard whenever the reciprocal relations of utilitarian social systems achieve mechanical efficiency, though the standard is problematic in these respects: Is an action moral if habit or good design is its sufficient condition? Does its moral satisfaction also require conscious commitment to a relationship and the expectations of one's partners? Normativity doesn't require more than habit or commitment until an agent is asked to justify doing what he or she typically does. Only then does one summon a coherent recounting of details that explain one's duty: including one's task, the expectations of partners, and its advantage or meaning to them or oneself.

These are measures of worth or obligation whether systems are utilities only or communities with embedded utilities: babysitters have a role and with it a duty; but not the duty of an able parent. For there are degrees of merit or fault when duties are satisfied or ignored. Moral intensity is measured by the character of the relationship and the measure of success or failure. I know you were waiting for lunch; I promised to bring it, but forgot. You're annoyed but not much damaged. Duties are norms that regulate instrumental relations—parent to child, teacher to student—though some slide below the threat of harm to the risk of irritation. That's not surprising in the complexities of everyday life, where the mix of encounters and expectations—some consequential, others trivial—may seem boundless. Practical norms, like traffic laws, make complexity negotiable.

We expect variability in instrumental relationships: vital people are distracted or sick; machines don't work. We're less tolerant when collaboration is half-hearted because those failures are more likely construed as sabotage: you know she depends on you, but you walked away though she's six and you're sixty. Should commitment be vulnerable to a range of intensities? For if so, what is the point at which an agreement to cooperate lapses because the intention is too feeble to sustain a partnership? Do reciprocal duties lapse concurrently—you're no longer duty-bound because I won't perform as my role requires? Or does this train of thought embody the category mistake of supposing that duties derive from having roles while provoking expectations that they will be satisfied? For how could matters of fact (an *is*) entail a duty (an *ought*)?

Clarity comes with the realization that "category mistakes" often express semantic ossifications that obscure real differences. You, but not I, have duties to your parents, partners, children, and friends. Why am I exempt? Because these are not my parents, partners, children, or friends. Not participating in relationships that generate your duties saves me from sharing them. How were the duties formed? By the coupling of behavior or language indicating your intention and their expectations. Why are you bound by this coupling? Because you weren't dissembling, and because they took you literally. What more, what deontological thunderbolt is required to turn intention and expectation into the raw gold of duty?

Philosophy may insist that ordinary people err if they construe personal couplings and commitments as a sufficient condition for obligation, but what are people missing? Could it be that moral duty is untranslatable to a different form (money) until it acquires the weight of legal duty (you promised, implying a contract)? *Gesellschaft* societies are much more litigious than those of gemeinschaft, because initiative and competition provoke the discord appeased by lawyers and courts. But legal duties are conventional only, hence the paradox that formalizing the moral duties on which they're mounted cures moral ambiguity by converting it into legal fault. This distinction—legal or moral—requires the further distinction between alternate bases for legal fault: namely, violated conventions or moral harm (including bodily harm and agreements breached in transactions requiring mutual trust). Yet legal refinements are conventions that endlessly complicate charges of moral fault by distracting from violated duties, or by creating the myriad formal obligations and faults that overlay a bureaucratized society. Parking tickets and procedural failures are not the examples from which to generalize when peering through thickets of legal paper to discern relevant duties or faults. Cooperation is vital to much we do; its breaches are more than an inconvenience. Cruelty isn't purged of moral fault when punished by courts.

Cooperation among Communities

Communities-of-interest—utilities—are rarely self-sufficient. They have economic needs essential to their survival and successes; they need political skills appropriate to their interests and situations. Both are intensified by circumstances. Thinking of social complexity, we often restrict ourselves to the swathe of individuals as they move, like ocean currents, in ways that are alternately coherent or opposed. Those motions are also common to communities, though their encounters are complicated by their hierarchical relations, as when a family's prerogatives are subordinate to those of community health or its church.

Cooperation is the soothing intervention that averts conflict. We achieve it by identifying the essential interests of others and ourselves, while staying calm amid provocations. The negotiations required may be various because relevant considerations are specific to the issue at hand: neighbors, work, or school, international or domestic. They are also dense because every community survives within an ecology where space or resources are scarce. Goodwill reduces the friction of contending systems, while rules, like traffic laws, facilitate compromise. Add skills for assembling coalitions and negotiating with communities averse to compromise or opposed to the interests one defends. Complexities ramify when frustration in any one negotiation is intensified by irresolution in others. One loses sight of the costs entrained when conflict seems the easier solution.

COMMUNITIES-OF-ACCORD AND THEIR LAWMAKERS

Communities-of-accord establish the ambience and ground rules for assembly. Societies of both gemeinschaft and gesellschaft regard rules, laws, and standardized procedures as a condition for community formation; they don't agree that formulating and enforcing these norms is itself an exercise in cooperation. Those of gemeinschaft require that collaborations proceed on terms they specify. Flexible gesellschaft emphasizes voting, minority rights, and other democratic procedures; accord is slower to come but more likely to be consensual when it happens. It wants cooperation in law-making, and community formation and performance, but expects competition. Rousseau's *Social Contract* describes generic steps in a process surely fraught at every step. Think of the frontier as it resisted law in Kansas or Missouri. Accord was achieved—households, churches, and schools survived—because cooperation in defense of communities is as much a natural social inclination and norm as any we know.

Conflict

The conflicts concerning us are of nine kinds: (1) personal disputes between or among community members competing for status, rank, or some other advantage; (2) conflicts among a community's members regarding its aims, procedures, benefits, or their individual duties; (3) members conflicted when duties to one community require ignoring or deferring duties to another; (4) conflicts of duty to oneself versus duties to one's communities or their other members; (5) communities conflicted when their aims exceed their means; (6) communities disrupted by conflicting religious or political ideologies; (7) communities disputing their duties, costs, or benefits within a network; (8) conflicts among unrelated communities competing for opportunities, personnel, or resources; and (9) conflicts generated when latent communities-at-large (sects) awaken, organize, and fight to control their terrain.

Personal disputes between or among community members competing for status, rank, or some other advantage. A system's members compete for roles or benefits, sabotaging those to whom they're hostile or indifferent. Some systems may perform to a high standard if skilled people suppress their differences at critical moments, though hostility often reduces a system's performance before chronic friction kills it. Why do members stay in relationships they suffer? Principally because of complacency and habit or because of needing work or companions they can't replace. Systems adjust when other members take up the slack or—as in friendship or marriage—they break.

Conflicts among a community's members regarding its aims, procedures, benefits, or their individual duties. Which side bends when rigidly defined roles or plans challenge members whose skills or sensibilities are out of kilter with their demands? Or when a community's aim is unacceptable to members who negotiate, adapt, or leave? Conflict's effects within a system—whether a community-of-interest or -meaning—are easily disguised if it limps on, while damaged members are too weak or frightened to speak. Gemeinschaft covers its trail with holist moralizing, inertia, or intimidation. Gesellschaft discourages complaints: leave if you're unhappy. Contention is disguised because each system is a secret cave from the perspective of every other; looking too closely is perceived as intrusive.

Members conflicted when duties to one community require ignoring or deferring duties to another. Conflicted duties paralyze the individuals having them; systems are stymied by their irresolute members. When two friends need assistance, which one do you help? What does one say to an employer when there is work to do, though a child is home needing care? There is no formula for solving conflicts like these; one plays for time, dividing resources in useful ways, hoping for sympathy or relief. But there is no relief if money put aside for rent averts a fine by paying a tax bill. Wealth lubricates some conflicts, but not those of people attending Yankee-Mets games while fans of both. Gesellschaft sometimes resembles walking through swampy terrain after dark, never seeing the alligator until a bird squawks or a branch snaps: many choices, but no way to make them cohere in all situations.

Conflicts of duty to oneself versus duties to one's communities or their other members. Holism—gemeinschaft—avers that duties to the whole—the church, state, family, or team—have precedence over duties to oneself; pluralist gesellschaft reverses the order of priority. Forswearing a final solution, we consider the details of each contested situation: What is required by my duties to others and why is it required? What do I require and why? Answers and resolutions are as distinctive as the situations considered, though there is often something undecidable about choices that oppose a personal interest to those of valued others.

Communities conflicted when their aims exceed their means. Aims outrun means for want of personnel, resources, or circumstances. Communities struggle to narrow the one or augment the other, though aims reduced to means often seem paltry, and not worth the effort.

Communities disrupted by conflicting religious or political ideologies. Ideologies are views of reality organized and filtered by values. Gemeinschaft and gesellschaft are principal examples. Why couldn't we dispense with prisms such as these while seeing things as they are? Because society is a determinable—its features are generic rather than specific until they are made determinate by the imposition of a design. Discord is seismic because it disrupts the equilibrium established by a

122 Community

consensual community-of-accord. How is discord managed: autocratically or by a plan that divides resources and benefits? Does the quarrel rankle because there is no resolution?

Communities disputing their duties, costs, or benefits within a network. Some disputes are honest misunderstandings; agreements were vague; circumstances have changed. Others express the opportunism of agreements disciplined only by law when a partner has no regard for its commitment to another or the other's well-being. Gemeinschaft punishes these disputes by humiliating one or both parties: one or the other sins by breaking trust. Gesellschaft's moral lessons aren't as effective, because people familiar with bad faith are cynical about the force of its indictments.

Conflicts among unrelated communities competing for opportunities, personnel, or resources. These are familiar points of dispute. A holist society expects deference when it assigns resources; pluralist societies expect the competition they get. Politics is, ideally, the process of reducing hostility on the way to achieving compromises that enable contending communities to go their way while relating peaceably to competitors. Rancor is reduced when resources are widely available or when procedures and rules adjudicating their distribution are perceived as fair. But this is rarely the situation: resources are often scarce; practices and rules that seem natural because traditional favor some communities at a cost to others.

The ninth of these points is more detailed.

Conflicts generated when latent communities-at-large (sects) awaken, organize, and fight to control their terrain. A dominant regime—a religion or state—suffocates conflict by suppressing competing interests or points of view; all are folded into its social economy, everyone accepts its edicts and whatever benefits are distributed. That was gemeinschaft when conviction or the threat of punishment induced the semblance of unanimity. That time is past in many places. Take the bus or subway, enjoy reliable service while rarely seeing a familiar face. Speed and convenience, anomie and diversity characterize societies organized for efficiency and choice. Diversity is desirable if it means a variety of sensibilities and the productive tension generated by disparate aims and abilities. Yet diversity and scarcity are combustibles guaranteeing

COOPERATION AND CONFLICT

that resources and opportunities will be disputed in a society that prizes competition and initiative. We are litigious because conflict is guaranteed among aggressive people and systems, and because courts are responsible for settling our disputes.

Competition is several things: creative when it provokes better ways to pursue better aims; destructive when it damages benign competitors; vicious if loss means humiliation: murderous when sects defend identities and ideals aggrandized by myths. These increments exceed the tolerance of moderate sensibilities: we understand discord in societies where freedom and ample resources incite competition for advantage; we're puzzled by rancor. Is there a test confirming that the Yankees are more worthy than the Red Sox, evidence that one religious narrative is true while every other is false? Organized sports suppress hostility by holding competitions that decide a champion in the games of any season; this is a practical solution to conflicts generated intentionally—cosmetically, one wants to say—by siting teams in principal cities. Other disputes, including those generated by more elemental needs, also have rational solutions: the fair division of essential resources—access to food, clothing, and housing, for example—is achieved by equalizing vital means. But what's to be said of health and education: are they luxuries properly allotted to the wealthy; or basic needs distributed in accord with a leveling norm? Other disputes are quarrels about meaning: every sect has partisans convinced that their story is best, and that contenders, worse than false, are bogus or contemptible.

Disparities are controlled in differing ways. Inequalities are corrected by distributing opportunities and resources more equitably; people frustrated after losing a fair competition collect themselves before trying again. Conflicts founded in meaning (feeling, idealization, and purpose) are different: they resist practical cures because each side sees reality from within a narrative it refuses to justify or yield. But this, too, is an impasse with a solution. Let New York City be our example. Many of its people are secular—they profess no religious affiliation—while others have a sturdy religious identity. The city has ethnic restaurants that prefigure the diversity of its churches, synagogues, mosques, and temples. Estimates vary, but there are, as of this writing, roughly 200,000 Hindus, 65,000 Buddhists, 750,000 Muslims, 1,500,000 Jews, 5,000,000

124 COMMUNITY

Christians, with smaller fractions for residents of other religions. There are cities where the solution to difference would be war, yet New York—a religious plenum—is devoid of open religious conflict. There are partisans who say privately that theirs is the true religion, but this isn't a sentiment hawked from the towers of their churches and temples. Why? Because inhibition is one of education's effects in a society where governance is constitutionally secular.

Residents with religious convictions negotiate civil and commercial contracts in a legal space that is only secular (though some are enforceable in religious courts). That bias is consolidated when religious studies—taught at many secular colleges and universities—are organized as classes in comparative religion, not as opportunities for religious instruction. The occasional violence against religious people is quickly condemned by all sects before it descends into tribal war. This effect—sectarian differences neutralized—is a principal condition for the creation of civil societies. Those are communities of mutual tolerance or respect, societies in which difference is acknowledged and grievances rankle, without provoking violence. Calling their differences *aesthetic* or *metaphoric* annoys people loyal to a religion or ideology because all are committed to their faith or faction. But language is the rhetorical device of societies that neutralize religious or political difference as surely as they idealize the diversity of their ethnic restaurants. The result is an extraordinary social achievement. People freely lobby or worship as they wish, while detoxifying conflicts that once set people at one another's throats.

Conflicts of meaning are manageable, as many cities confirm. Their diversity, coupled to pragmatism and generations of secular education, make them resistant to monolithic views about this life or any to come. But old meanings agitate myriad hostilities. For meaning is significance: the feelings, values, and motives constitutive of one's beliefs and practices, the metaphysical design one ascribes to reality. Each is the illumination internal to communities where speculation has grown beyond the need for safety, order, and material means. Each is the signature expressing a community's sense of authenticity and purpose, the sustaining backdrop to practical lives. Meanings control motives, understandings, and feelings; they dictate social practices and the manner of interpersonal relations. Yet meanings—feelings, idealizations, aims—construed dogmatically as truths and norms are a menace to social peace. Isolated communities, each enforcing its code on all residents, may be coherent and self-sustaining in favorable circumstances. But two or more communities, each formed to the requirements of meanings that are mutually anomalous and intolerant, cannot tranquilly occupy the same space.

Grievances, like meanings, are often schismatic. Communities-at-large are latent when these complexities are suppressed by full-employment economies, tolerant societies, and efficient political management. But this circle of conditions is rare. People motivated to find reasons for their disadvantages are sensitive to their differences: ethnicity, race, and gender are some principal markers. Inequalities rankle because of inequities and because they often express diminished respect, sometimes contempt for their victims. Abused people recover pride and an intensified sense of their distinguishing properties, when consciousness feeds solidarity. Those aroused and organized are better able to defend themselves when challenging dominant castes or clans. *Sectarianism* is synonymous with *communitarianism* when communities confront one another because members are suffused with meanings or grievances and interests that are or seem mutually exclusive. Imagine neighbors who share a taste for loud music, though each assaults the thin walls dividing them with music despised by the other. Extrapolate to religions that fill the intellectual and moral space with mutually unacceptable narratives. There are analogues at every scale: from high school cliques and the fans of opposing teams to ethnicities and states. Each is a faction whose members bond with intensities that rise in proportion to the real or imagined slights of a provocative other. Each may suppose that its dominanc would be evidence of truth and entitlement.

Sectarian conflict is the domestic analogue for foreign wars. The engine promoting it is the mix of grievances, anomalous meanings, fear, hatred, and competition. Difference alone is benign if space and resources are ample; scarcity makes it fraught, though resources and practical interests may be secondary if meaning is primary. The challenge is existential: cure our grievance; make your meaning prevail, and you efface our truth, our identity. We resist with whatever violence is required for our survival. Will you acknowledge us? Not if that requires sacrificing your advantages or conceding our right to affirm a view different from yours. Is there any way to suppress this storm? Only a victory so complete that the other side is destroyed. Martin Heidegger expressed his solution in 1940.

> "Constructive" thought is at the same time "exclusive." In this way it fixes and maintains what can support the edifice and fends off what endangers it. In this way it secures the foundation and selects the building materials. Constructive-exclusive thought is simultaneously "annihilative." It destroys whatever stoppages and restraints hinder the constructive rising to the heights. Annihilation offers security against the pressure of all conditions of decline. Construction demands exclusion. Every constructing (as a creating) embraces destruction.[1]

> Will to power, the essential complex of enhancement of power and preservation of power, brings its own essence to power, that is, to appearance in beings, by empowering itself for overpowering. Will to power is representation that posits values. Yet construction is the supreme mode of enhancement. Differentiating and conserving exclusion is the supreme mode of presentation. Annihilation is the supreme mode of counteressence of preservation and enhancement.[2]

> The essence of truth that all metaphysics assumes and preserves—even if it is still in total oblivion—is a letting appear. It is the revealing of what is concealed. It is unconcealment. Thus "justice" because it is the supreme mode of will to power is the proper ground for the determination of the essence of truth. In the metaphysics of the absolute and consummate subjectivity of will to power truth occurs essentially as justice.[3]

These are passages from the section titled "Justice" in *Nietzsche*, volume 3, Heidegger's formulation of Nietzsche's view. "Justice," as Heidegger construed it, may require annihilating the alien other, though the sectarianism for which he wrote doesn't entail bilateral conflict: it's sufficient that one side ruin the other.

Are there less murderous solutions? Two ways of disarming sectarian antagonisms are versions of triangulation. One mediates antagonisms from a position neutral to the point disputed, while encouraging both sides to accept a resolution honestly adjudicated. Yet accommodation doesn't work if hostilities are founded in legitimate grievances or the anomalous meanings shaping incommensurable views of reality. For, then, compromise implies a lack of confidence in the truth of one's beliefs about matters construed as sacred or merely practical but life sustaining. The other resolution is abstract. Identify, for example, the beliefs and practices of a worldview acceptable to both sides: call it Y. Then ease the way to Y by replacing contrary views of reality with one or the other of middle terms—A or B—each entailing Y. Resolution comes if both sides achieve Y—one by way of A, the other by way of B. Negotiation succeeds if each concedes that the competitor favors beliefs and practices admired by both. But this is complex in ways making it unlikely to succeed.

What's to be done when negotiations fail? That happens if they're centered on intellectual solutions to conflicts rooted in loyalties and feelings. There is little or no common ground when sects are distinguished by cultures that dispute reality's character or its significance for beliefs, rights, and morals. Negotiations are poisoned by competitors that ignore a sect's grievances or ridicule its history. There may be no neutral positions from which to arbitrate these conflicts; and no meanings that suppress conflicts by sublating them. (This should be a warning to marketeers excited by the promise of selling virtual realities. Their success might promote endless virtual worlds—each with its distinctive culture; each unintelligible to others in worlds where "justice" has different meanings and conditions.)

People are often in a hurry, though drivers observe traffic laws without regarding the laws as devious forces or other drivers as enemies. Hostility would dissipate if affect and meaning were to resemble enthusiasms that come and go, but that isn't a prospect where sects challenge one another to right their grievances or endorse their justifying narratives. The grievances may be real; the narratives prefigure tribal identities. Add that each sect responds to sneering others with the massed ferocity of its members. All this might be suppressed by a constraining loop—irony, prudence, or laughter—but there may be no negative feedback if neither sect is embarrassed or restrained when hating the other. We counsel people to be reasonable; concede that cultures are variable, that ingredients are often the same though we cook them differently. Allow that other beliefs are possible and that yours may be mistaken; consider that fantasy isn't truth and that passion isn't evidence that it is. But irony and inhibition aren't available to people for whom belief and practice are marks of loyalty and identity: I am what I believe and do. Secularism promotes itself as an antidote to sectarian anger. But what is one to do when secular scruples are alien to sects dominated by real grievances or global mythologies? Secularists assume that resentful people can learn the tolerance of productive societies if they acquire secure places within them. But what if there is no social engine promising integration and opportunity to the disfavored? What is the secular solution to chronic violence?

Thomas Hobbes faced this issue during a civil war when life and sanity favored suppressing the violence. One needn't agree with his view of autocracy to concede that one solution to civil war is a power sufficient to stop it. Yet this, too, is problematic if the intervening power is the politically empowered version of a contending side: quelling the violence could motivate a suicidal last stand. Hobbes's solution works best if government stands apart from its hostile sects, allowing each to perceive it as neutral in matters opposing them. Baroque operas call down authorizing bolts of lightning; we're satisfied by constitutional prerogatives that enable intervention when sectarian violence breaches social peace.

Success may nevertheless elude a governing authority for any of three reasons: (1) Eliminating disparities doesn't erase the effects of meaning; communities that affirm different ideas of reality are mutually unintelligible, unless there is a common secular language and an idea of justice or rights to which each defers. (2) Hegemonic communities—those dominating governance and the economy—aren't strongly motivated to concede space or power. They construe the weakness of subordinate communities as evidence that their complaints are more rhetorical than real. (3) Weaker communities aren't likely to see government's interventions as expressions of neutral goodwill if its authority expresses the interests and will of a dominant community. That persuasion is often accurate.

Suppose nevertheless (and for want of better solutions) that a state tries to suppress communal hostilities by recourse to its laws and police power. That, by itself, is sometimes a cure: people living peaceably together discover the comity they once resisted, with the effect that law is no longer required to enforce an effect they enjoy. But then hostilities surge and people again feel justified destroying their neighbors. One imagines a future psychotropic gas that reduces conflict by suppressing different points of view. But who wields the power to use it? And how do we decide which differences to suppress? Formulating an effective agent may be only a matter of time; solving the social problems is more elusive.

Chapter Six

The One and the Many

The One and the many is an ontological puzzle, but also the expression of conflicted thinking about autonomy and socialization. The phrase is rightly construed in either of three ways. Traditionally, but incidentally here, the One is essence or Form, and the many are its instantiations. More pertinent because apt to distract us, the One is the cosmos or God while the many are myriad particulars arrayed within it. Or, with equal plausibility, the One is every community or agent as it negotiates a society where its interests or needs are alternately satisfied or frustrated by others or by an aspect of society at large The cosmic One embodies everything actual within itself; social Ones—individuals, systems, networks, and societies—are only relatively self-sufficient.

Causal Analysis

The social One—all of humanity—is splintered by myriad people, their systems, and networks. Its complexity is provocative: are systems whole in name only because their parts are members having freedom of action; or is autonomy nominal because, as in gemeinschaft, all submit to the logic of the whole (like dancers performing a choreographer's steps)? Wanting an explication responsive to the dynamics of systems, and to ideas accessible in English, I use the traditional but accurate language of efficient and formal cause. It contrasts the relative autonomy of

132 COMMUNITY

individuals with designs for community formation. Individuals want freedom of action: thinking, doing, or making on terms of their own. Yet systems of any scale subordinate individual autonomy when their designs—like a piano's eighty-eight keys or the rules of a game—restrict the range of one's actions. Causal language is intelligible to readers, and useful, too, because it acknowledges the normative geography of social systems. More than *is*, it records the *should*s or *must*s requiring members to satisfy their systems' rules or roles: "Vote," "Don't cross," "Move." This is more nuance and more ontology than a mereology using set theory can easily express. Its syntax supplies representations of a many integrated by logical operators, but not the character of the unifier, its unifying act, or those it integrates. More than a succinct representation of unity, we want to understand the entities unified and the act or process of their integration.

People resist using causal terms to describe community because mechanical language often overlays the experience of a One made intelligible by metaphoric religious or ideological language with talk of parts, causal relations, and design. But these are discrepancies in rhetoric, alternate ways of construing a single complexity. Simple examples—friendships or the contractual relations of buyer and seller—confirm that causes are sufficient for the formation of social systems and our experience of their effects. Assume, for example, that community is a partnership, and that nothing is accomplished without members who engage one another in variably demanding reciprocities: You wash, I'll dry; sell it and I'll pay. These are agents mutually affected when acting together; the activities are variable; their causal structure is identical whatever the example, its scale, or complexity. Associations are also causal: I believe because all my family and friends are believers; their conviction dispels my doubts.

Integrated or Contained

In its pantheist reading, the One is God, a container for the finite many created within it. How God creates the many is usually ignored because unknown. The cosmos—how nature differentiates and stratifies itself—is better known. But God and the cosmos are alike in the respect that each is construed as a receptacle for the many they integrate. Circumstances are reversed for social Ones: we see the birth and education of persons, and the assembly of social systems. Communities-at-large usually precede us, but their changes are chronicled and sometimes explained. A phrase that provokes theological imaginations[1]—the One and the many—is also a research project for biologists and social scientists. What do they study? The formation of social units: persons, social systems, their networks, and societies.

We don't know how a god would integrate the many (perhaps by thinking of them as one); but we do know the designs and causal reciprocities responsible for the functional unity of human bodies, social systems, and their networks. Friendship emerges when two people address and respond to one another with mutual affection, interest, and respect. Feelings, habits, and reliably satisfied expectations explain its tensile strength. Variables like these account for the unity of social entities throughout the scale from individuals to systems, networks, and communities-at-large. But unity is harder to create and sustain as competitive duties or the number of participants augments: a reliable worker neglects a task because of responsibilities at home; two friends compete for the attention of a third. Oneness is often imperfect or unachieved because exceptions to unity are commonplace. God and the cosmos seem unproblematically One; *e pluribus unum* eludes us.

Moral Coherence

Gemeinschaft translates as *community*; what more is implied when community is the One? That dignity and worth are mutually affirmed within the whole overseen by God or informed by the Good, that the personal experience of meaning—significance—adumbrates the ample One in which all human interests find their expression: "The more pathways are provided for participation in diverse ways and touching multiple interests—for example, worshiping in Catholic churches, attending Catholic schools, contributing to Catholic charities, reading the Catholic press—the richer is the experience of community."[2]

134 Community

Convictions that illumine one's tasks and relations galvanize many people; others resist the theology or ideology this requires. Ideas of gesellschaft don't require a grand rationale because the communities they acknowledge vary in size, composition, and purpose, and because aversion to figurative language is one of its motives. Gesellschaft is blithe; it doesn't acknowledge spiritual unity or the cosmic Good. It prefers diversity to unity: do what you like while taking care that others aren't damaged by your actions. Every community-of-interest or -meaning is nevertheless a One relative to its members. Each is a moment in the history of the community-at-large—the society—in which it forms.

The society, too, isn't freestanding; it trades with others and survives on Earth's surface. Is that ecosystem—humanity in nature—the true One, or is it the larger scale in which Earth rotates the Sun at a distance favorable to life? Where the cosmos is the only One, we make distinctions that are more than conventional because the unities considered have structural and functional integrity, and some freedom of motion within their contexts. Both social systems emphasized here—communities-of-interest and communities-of-meaning—have this freedom within gesellschaft, and to a lesser degree within gemeinschaft. Meaning emerges when a utility's efficiency is abetted by the affinity of its members. The utility surviving within the community functions as before, while fellowship enhances worker relationships when each addresses others as persons, not as functionaries having identities that reduce to their roles. We invoke *community* for its implication that people are to be regarded as ends, not only as means. Communities, this implies, are moral Ones: they have duties to members committed to their aims, to bystanders, and to the society from which they draw resources. Duty may be the principal, if implicit, referent in many of the word's social uses. Almost everyone participates in several or many communities, hence the sense, maybe the anxiety, that duties to them can't be alienated.

Contrary Inclinations

Uniformity stabilized by divine sanction or cosmic design contests the scrappy initiatives of people who don't need Platonic architecture or

THE ONE AND THE MANY   135

a god's approval. Yet this polarity—aversion to dissent and a passion for unity versus tolerant plurality—ignores the dialectical tension that binds them. These are contrary inclinations that course through our social arrangements; like an alternating current, each provokes the other in offsetting cycles. Unifying gemeinschaft relieves anxiety until we're annoyed by too much coherence; welcoming gesellschaft and freedom, we ignore the whiff of incipient friction. Community can't break this cycle if each of its two strokes is alternately provoked, then repelled, by the idea of the other. Bored by perpetual peace, we fear that discord is a late step on the way to violence. Neither phase masters its circumstances because each is sabotaged by an attractor that promises to cure its faults.

Will the One or Ones of a social domain be unitary or fractured and dispersed? The issue is joined but unresolved in each of these domains: (1) locale, (2) polity, (3) economy, (4) culture, and (5) species.

Locale. Locale in a social domain is one of three things: position within a system of interest or meaning; relative position in a network of systems; or location within one of alternate possible communities-of-accord (disciplinary spaces).

Relative position in a community-of-interest or -meaning confirms that community has emerged when members have bonded for a common aim: rather than imagining playing a game, they've joined a team. Their familiarity is qualified in electronic neighborhoods where initiatives are launched by people having sketchy knowledge of one another. Yet the original assumption—that we bond to people trusted because known—is accurate when trust is founded in emotional responses evoked by face-to-face interactions, though rarely by the internet or electronic texts. This is pertinent, as well, for one's choice of disciplinary spaces: How much familiarity does one want? How much can one tolerate? Gemeinschaft promises companions who share its values, including corporate control of one's choices. The people of gesellschaft expect that others will respect one another's differences or at least their right to be different. Forming communities obliges us to choose between these ideas of a moral One.

Their similarities ambiguate that choice. We reasonably assume that urban densities are reliable contexts for meeting others, and that urban centers are the higher-order social Ones enabling those encounters. Each is a gemeinschaft or gesellschaft of greater or smaller scale, and each is distinguished by norms that galvanize or discourage the formations of certain communities: the Vatican has requirements for the recognition of new priestly orders; laissez faire is the energizer in other cities. The distinction of fore- and background is, however, tricky. Imagine the gas clouds in which stars form. City density is their imperfect analogue: gas clouds predate their stars, though neighborhoods can't predate their houses and residents. Urbanity is a textured web of expectations; people feel its rhythms as they move within it. The ethos is holistic and subtly prescriptive, yet open and pluralistic. Gesellschaft's opposition to gemeinschaft would seem paradoxical or irrelevant to residents who move freely while living in what they experience as a space that's filled, though not closed. This is gesellschaft with some of the comforts essential to gemeinschaft. The moral Ones of urban experience are, to this degree, merged.

Now consider that the Ones of social life are hierarchically ordered within their disciplinary spaces. An extended family is sometimes backdrop to its constituent nuclear families; a manufacturing or financial center welcomes businesses with interest or skills like or complementary to its own. This complexity—foreground communities abetted by larger-scale communities of their kind—is a condition for the proliferation of communal networks: young families in the context of their intergenerational molecular families; banking in Frankfurt, London, or New York. This is an irony in the Oneness of gesellschaft: describing it as a permissive open space deprives it of substance it doesn't acquire until, like gemeinschaft, it fills with collaborating people and systems. Add that spaces of both kinds are organized hierarchically. Each higher order is a rule or condition having regulative force on the one immediately below: persons within systems within networks within ecologies, regions, and beyond. One is totalizing, the other open and tolerant at its lower orders, but in this respect, their realizations are similar.

Polity. A regulative weave is a One that enables choices and actions while limiting preferences in a constitutionally ordered society. Like contract or traffic laws, it directs behavior when choice or action risks damage to those engaged. This is polity as it limits the initiatives undertaken within it; each has a regulative signature that shapes the actions and moral sentiments of its residents. Polities vary, with the result that the people and systems of one may be stymied by challenges for which those of another have solutions.

We assume that a polity's rules are calculated to encourage the formation of social systems making it safe and productive in ways appropriate to its aims. But the values of some autocracies are averse to any formation that may challenge their authority. States with that bias are likely to punish initiatives others reward, though community formation is stultified if one can't know how any initiative will evolve. Fear becomes the shroud paralyzing changes of all sorts. These societies wait and die.

Economy. Economies, like polities, are variable: do they encourage the formation of social systems or is wealth captive to those who fear that sharing it would reduce their well-being? This anxiety is itself a background condition, one whose intensities affect community initiatives. A strong economy promotes their formation: people comfortable in themselves look for ways to find companions with whom to share tastes, moral causes, and experiments. Despotic polities make friendship dangerous because a nominal friend might prove to be a government spy; poor economies discourage the formation of families if couples fear that employment is too precarious to support a household, let alone the welfare of children. Gesellschaft embarrasses itself when the competition of its plutocrats intensifies; benign communities can't form or—like plants deprived of water—they collapse when people dominating wealth or political power see themselves as survivors in a perpetual civil war. They fear, with their own vindictiveness as evidence, that any concession to the welfare of others will vitiate their well-being. Birth rates plunge, society shrinks.

Culture. Culture is a One that penetrates every social practice; it integrates tastes and behavior while interests and needs mold its utilities and communities. Culture is pervasive without implying that it's monolithic: people don't always wear the same clothes; restaurants don't have the same menus. Nativism fears impurity, though we learn to discount responses that are hegemonic rather than aesthetically discerning. Our access to information about disparate cultures alters

138 COMMUNITY

the nativist effect by extending the array of one's choices; we're cosmopolitan rather than parochial, but still cloistered within the space infiltrated by styles and values different from the one called "home." The freedom to go one's cultural way is fiercely defended, but without liberating us from culture's control. For culture is a plenum; there may be no aspect of life unaffected by it.

Sensibility requires time; we educate ourselves by looking and listening, though we're often slow to adjust because novelty is hard to read or because we need better rubrics for integrating exotic affects. Or the sequence is reversed: culture alters because novelty and initiative challenge sensibility and established styles. Tested by matters or events we can't decipher, we experiment; communities catch up when familiarity turns an exotic import into a teachable style. This is the paradox that a cultural One may be complete at any time (because each of its variables has a value) while changeable and likely changing.

Species. There is an idea of the human community founded in our interdependence and the powers common to us; or we invoke DNA and the fact that each of us could, with some exceptions, reproduce with one of the other sex. These realizations, with speculation that humans are descended from one or a few women in long-ago Africa, fuels the idea that we are offshoots of a single root. This idea of species grounds the moral force ascribed to the human community. We imagine being responsible to and for one another, because *ought*, we suppose, has its origin in a biological *is*. The inference is consequential because it provides missing leverage when there seems a compelling reason for averting preventable disparities: let each of us acknowledge the resonant sensibility in every person imagined or encountered.

Now join locale, polity, economy, and culture to species: is that sufficient to create the layered but integrated One recognizable by all? A sociologist of great conceptual power might produce an idea of society sufficiently subtle to make an intelligible One of this complexity. Gemeinschaft struggles with this challenge; its proponents invoke God or the Good, each a way of arousing emotions, idealizations, and purposes—meanings—that disguise our failure to discern unity in the diversity we experience. Is there a meaning—emotion or interpretation—likely to create the impetus for a unitary society? Its features are unpredictable, though it will probably be motivated, if ever it comes, by a theistic or ideological instinct for salvation in people despairing amid clutter or disruption.

Control

The One and the many prefigures the difference between gemeinschaft and gesellschaft: the first unifies the many while containing it; the other provides space for the many while making minimal claims on them. The difference seems bald and irreconcilable, though it isn't because their contrariety is softened by the rigor embodied in a society that has learned to satisfy its needs in laws and practices appropriate to its physical circumstances and resources. How does it house, feed, and defend itself? Do risks to stability make it severely literal or more accommodating; are people more leery of stasis or disruption? Tönnies's 1887 book expressed his anxiety about disruption's effects on settled German ways.

> And only since and insofar as man generally and essentially has become a subject, must the question as a result for him become explicit, as to whether man as the arbitrarily shrunken and willfully released "I" or as the "we" of society—as individual or as community, as a personality in the community or as simple group member of the corporate body, as state and nation or as a people—will and must become the subject that he, *as* a modern being, already *is*. Only where man is essentially already a subject is there the possibility of his slipping into the un-being of "subjectivity" in the sense of "individualism" But it is also only there, where man remains a subject, that the explicit struggle *against* individuality and *for* the community as the target field of all accomplishment and advantage has new meaning.[3]

Personal differences were acceptable in terms of Tönnies's idea of gemeinschaft, though he seemed ambivalent about an idea of autonomy common to Rousseau and Mill: that each person should cultivate the intellect and sensibility to be acquired within a community that enriches the distinctive talents of its members.[4]

Tinkering with Germany's disciplinary space in the style of democratic politics (Weimar, for example) might have resolved tribal anxieties and conflicts over time, but Tönnies, like Heidegger, might have been impatient. Democratic communities, each sensitive to the principle that we should live and let live, encourage diversity by respecting it. But this is gesellschaft, a formation that renounces ideals of tribal purity. Losing the will to realize and disclose their spiritual essence, Heidegger's people believed themselves infiltrated and debased by lesser tribes. Hence, the zeal for annihilation: let murder reduce the cosmopolitan pressure his people seemed unable to resist.

Unity by Way of a Narrative

Are there other ways to create a social One? Consider, with James's *Varieties of Religious Experience* as our point of reference, the isolation and singularity of psychological states that evolve, when socialized, into the signature narrative of a religion or ideology. Its initial data are idiopathic: singular, neurotic, and incommunicable. Evoking an elevated degree of emotional intensity, they intimate a reality or ideal different from those of practical life or scientific understanding. And critically, these experiences are a many, never a One, because each is prelinguistic and inexpressible. This, according to James, is the beginning of religion, not its sputtering end, for the intensity of the experience drives affected people to seek the understanding of companions. Language enables the mutual understanding achieved by shared rituals and a story that specifies a reality whose exalted status would explain the mystery intimated by each of the many private experiences. It is here, with shared beliefs, practices, and communicable meanings—ritual, songs, and the narrative—that the many become One. This happens, though its motivating experiences fall outside the perimeter of mutual understanding. We suppress or forget the original awareness, defending socialization, when our new assets—a narrative, habits, beliefs, and

THE ONE AND THE MANY   141

rituals—are public surrogates for the barely discernible content and emotional conviction that impelled its first witnesses.

Many of the religiously faithful would have learned its beliefs and practices as children, without the singular experiences that first impelled adherence to their sect's social forms. But that was its origin, never its social content. Believers sometimes try to recover those provoking moments in prayer, meditation, dance, song, or speaking in tongues; but efforts fail because the first impulses were singular. Recovering them would guarantee frustration because people would be, as before, unable to comprehend or communicate their content. Language makes the many a One, requiring all the while that they look past the experiences that first excited religious belief.

People aroused, but mutually unintelligible, might despair that no one understands them. Why should they defer? Because those having rituals, beliefs, and a story are a militant army, a community-of-meaning that willingly challenges skeptics who don't concede the significance of their stories and beliefs. Both sides want vindication, acknowledgment that their experiences are veridical perceptions of the transcendent. Yet the character of religious experience is radically altered by the gap between these two: the first is singular, unknown to others, and unintelligible to the subject having it; the second is communicable because socialized while having no discernible link to its motivating experience. How is the socialized second vindicated by the singular first? Why believe that religious symbols and rituals are appropriate to the many undecipherable experiences? There is no reason, though language and community nurture belief.

Reality Testing

Social Ones—whether spiritual or ideological—may be tested in either or both of two ways: are there decidable experiments that justify confidence in the truth of their beliefs, or is their coherence generated by the credulity of their members and the grammar of their stories? Many social utilities (hospitals and subways, people cured or safely carried) rightly claim evidence for their reality testing. But whole societies are

142 COMMUNITY

sometimes unified by their myths: no justification—no evidence for the truth of their beliefs—is required when emotion and convention testify to their coherence. A monument in Santa Clara, a neighborhood in Seville, memorializes the 114 people burnt at the stake in 1512 to save their souls. We expect children to outgrow their stories, but don't require as much from parents and their communities. Why? Because conviction and solidarity are more important to the faithful than beliefs justified by reality-testing: evidence and inference. This is characteristic of gemeinschaft but anathema to gesellschaft. Beliefs, aims and organization are testable: Do we achieve our aims? Is there evidence for our beliefs—do we win, are we cured—if not, why not?

Distance

Discussion above assumes that the One is a container or integrator, and that individuals are compliant when gathered within a One. Yet the One and the many may also be construed in this other way: the One is any individual distanced from the many for either of two reasons.

Reflection. Whether committed to a system or considering participation, one steps back to appraise it and one's motives for joining. This is autonomy, as it expresses the complementary powers of freedom to and from: members are entitled to appraise a system's costs and benefits. Participation may be coerced, but it requires, if voluntary, that it satisfy their interests and values. We're irreparably planted in moral terrains that are separable but linked: one is the array of systems chosen or inherited and affirmed; the other is one's calculating, moralizing self. Agents are empowered to doubt, deny, or refuse; they reserve the power to withdraw.

Anomie. A different reading of *the One* and the many observes that everyone is sometimes withdrawn from others. He or she is a One, intensely self-aware; they are remote. This may be the effect of Nietzschean autonomy—opportunistic or assertive—or it expresses illness, alienation, or depression. Émile Durkheim described the condition signified as *anomie* in 1893: societies changing as Tönnies described—from gemeinschaft to gesellschaft—extrude people from

THE ONE AND THE MANY   143

familiar disciplines and places. People disoriented when left behind may be unrecognizable to others and themselves.[5]

The word's meaning, as currently used, is generalized to signify people who distance themselves from the crowding and complexity of their surroundings. They're anxious and cautious, though knowledgeable about social or cultural changes and wealthy enough to enjoy those they approve. Living principally in big cities where the response to density, noise, or risk is social withdrawal, they're more likely to be witnesses than participants. Yet there is a chasm between self-willed distance and the anonymity of despair. Big cities are liable to both. Withdrawal is productive for artists and writers, though disoriented people are lost to others and themselves. Could we do more to save them? Some small societies reeducate workers whose jobs disappear when tasks, products, or services are superseded by an evolving economy. Cities that thrive on self-sufficiency are too careless to notice.

Opposed Hypotheses

Is a One created by relations binding ensembles of the many or are the many and their communities the precipitates emerging within an ontologically prior One? This is the difference between the One as the integrator of many, and the One as their self-differentiating creator. A creator God would be credited with powers for both, if we assume that it embodies the complex it makes. A high-energy space-time—self-differentiating (by generating properties) and self-stratifying (by generating tiers of hierarchically organized individuals and relationships)—may also be ontologically prior to qualifications that are distinguishable but not separable from it. Space, time, energy, motion, cause, and law may be the primordial variables from which all else is generated. (Matter/mass requires energy fields and the Higgs boson.)

Is it also possible that space and time, each on its own, is prior to their integration as space-time? That doesn't follow. They are distinguishable but not separable when motion presupposes their integration; each is a measure of motion's trajectory through the other: space of time, time of space. Is their separability conceivable in the absence of motion? One could plot the essential formal properties of each without regard for the other, proving that they are distinguishable, though not separable, given motion. Hume argued that everything distinguishable is separable, but that followed only because he reduced reality to percepts that are vivid and discrete. His phenomenalist assumptions explain our incomprehension when something critical—energy, for example—isn't reducible to a percept.

What conception would we have if Hume's principles were onto-logically decisive: would space be construed as an empty receptacle, time as duration without change? Each is conceivable, but why suppose that either is accurate to space or time itself? We perceive stability without change in phenomena undergoing changes that are rapid or spasmodic at orders of physical reality invisible to us. Duration without change, in them, is an illusion fostered by the relatively gross resolving power of human perception. The idea of empty space is both an abstraction and the apparent content of some perceptions: a vast blue sky. But this, too, is a failure of perception: we miss the detail. Are the abstractions—empty space, unruffled duration—more reliable? They have often been points of reference for traditional ideas of space and time, though they mislead us by implying a backdrop to events occurring within them—wind-blown clouds, people walking—rather than the media qualified by the energy and geometry of processes they embody. Yet change, energy exchange, and their products are, we speculate, the reality: space-time is their inseparable condition and determining context. Accordingly, there is a One—space-time—conceptually prior to its qualifications, though not separable or abstractable from them. Philosophy waits on physics to tell us how or why it diversifies itself.

This isn't the last word because there might be worlds—it's not a contradiction—in which there are space and time but no motion binding them by requiring both. That possibility is not our world.

Singularity

The social One is steeply hierarchical, with Ones atop each of its descending orders. First—because highest—is the aspirational community-of-accord, the moral hope that all may live in safety while enjoying well-being. This is ideally a domain that stretches wherever people live, though more realistically, we spread our aspiration no further than people controlling some degree of the conditions for their well-being. Accord's principal expressions, gemeinschaft or gesellschaft, are second order. Prescribing alternate ideas of well-being's organizational conditions, they are followed by particular societies, constituent communities, and persons. Aristotle (substance) and Descartes (the *cogito)* would say this skein is upside down: they would build up from individual bodies, minds, or persons. But our vantage point is community, first in its abstract, determinable form, then in its ever more determinate expressions.

This starting point is, however, problematic: does aspiration bear ontological weight. Is there anything substantial to the aspiration for community? It is substantial if community, more than a mode of organization or association, is a social attractor in human relations, a final cause—an ideal steady state—essential to the formation of uman sociality. I assume that communities form and stabilize when reciprocal causal relations bind members whose tasks are significant for some aspect of human welfare. Their relations aren't as tight as those of atoms in molecules or organs in bodies, but they are recognizable in friendship, utilities, and the bonds of citizens. Imagining that these wholes are reducible to their parts misconstrues them. Emergence creates Ones whose prime parts—cells, organs, bodies—are ever more loosely bound. But every such entity has coherence and integrity appropriate to its emergent order: rabbits don't reduce to rabbit parts, communities don't reduce to their members. Reciprocal causality and purpose are the difference.[6]

Perspective

The gap between social Ones and their members is perspectival: How far can I stand from fellow workers or neighbors without losing an identity that makes me recognizable to them? How close can I be without losing core properties vital to myself? The gap is moral because it raises

146 Community

questions about one's duties to others and oneself; it is political when challenging the legitimacy of those responsible for social coherence and public safety. Nietzsche may have believed that one can't get close to others without trading critical perspective for an amalgam of banalities. Thinking, feeling, or acting as others do, compromising judgment and sensibility, we capitulate to the herd. Its members may suppose that they retain vital powers, though all would have lost whatever abilities enabled them to make distinctions or appraisals different from those agreeable to the many.

How do we enjoy socialization while enriching sensibility and the likely realization that we're different from others? Community is the evocative solution: acknowledge one's partners in relationships where the work of all may depend on the singular skills and sacrifices of each. Incorporate every personal One into a welcoming many. The formula seems plain, though community eludes us. Why resist it? There's an answer in James's *Varieties* and Leibniz's *Monadology*: we're stubborn and competitive: but more, we're separate and sometimes mutually unintelligible. We're used to the company of others, but we're anxious or frightened and easily annoyed. A few would be self-sufficient if they could.

Cosmological speculations are compelling, but they're a distraction from the smaller scale of social reality: social systems versus members whose experiences, like the religious people of James's *Varieties*, are singular, even monadic. W. V. O. Quine likely favored measures of social uniformity, yet he acknowledged that language is individuating: "No two of us learn our language alike, nor in a sense, does any finish learning it while he lives."[7] One might suppose that rarely used words may be added to a language without revising its inferential structure. But Quine was a linguistic holist; adding stray words wasn't his concern. Given that each of us alters his or her associative linguistic networks throughout life, it follows that this principal mode of construing the world differs among us and differs over time in each of us. Socialization makes us mutually intelligible, but not transparent. In Quine as in James, we are always a many, never quite a One.

Afterword

Totalizing gemeinschaft creates community by assembling people to the demands of an a priori idea. Roles are decided by its design; managers are self-anointing. Everyone else devotes him- or herself to a role and the chance that its tasks are appropriate to one's talents. Gesellschaft does nothing comparable: it provides a neutral space and tolerance for uses that are peaceful and efficient. People reliably collaborate in utilities that satisfy essential needs, though gesellschaft's communities may be rudely competitive. Violence is deterred by laws and civic habits, but studied neutrality and the emphasis on opportunity deter communities-of-meaning. Like the open invitation to a dance floor—whichever steps you wish—its emphasis on self-sufficiency and advantage deters intimacy.

People who rue the loss of meaning often mourn the passing of gemeinschaft from the perspective of gesellschaft. Holism was comforting. Adherents had the solace of believing that everything pertinent to safety and prosperity was enabled by their disciplinary space. It promised salvation, while determining one's choices and beliefs. Equanimity was plausible there, though not so much in social spaces where each person is obliged to create a niche for him- or herself. Gesellschaft values initiative, skill, foresight, and staying power. It's suspicious of alliances that stifle opportunity or repress a personal inclination. But we're not all concert pianists; demands like those for which they're prepared are scary to people of scant means and little preparation. Mourning the holism, safety, and significance once ensured by a religion or regime, we fear having to create value and security out of talent, choice, and opportunity.

148   COMMUNITY

Enjoying liberty while often defeated in competitive societies with fragile safety nets, we retreat to our utilitarian systems. These are our principal communities and often, save for family, friends, or religious services, the only ones. We're demoralized without quite knowing why. Communities are the sites of personal discovery and the webs of our interdependence, yet motivation founders. Communities-of-interest are often commonplace and reliable because need impels us to make and sustain them. Communities-of-meaning don't rise above the horizon where they emerge as sentimental icons: the family, neighborhood, or school.

Cities are a partial solution. Those with prosperous economies reduce the contrariety of gemeinschaft and gesellschaft by joining holism to plurality: people working together are always nearby. Holistic in respect to laws and infrastructure, each city or town satisfies an array of tastes and talents. Contemporary life in them is often a plenum—with more to do than there's time for doing it—though with little in the way of common purpose or shared meanings. There, too, we're drawn in contrary ways. No flaneur knows the geography and mood of every neighborhood. Attachment is often fragile; many of us are mutually respectful loners. Gesellschaft—libertarian, pragmatic, and fallible—largely succeeds in its terms. We fault its emphatic instrumentalism, but want nothing that recalls the autocracy of its holist contrary.

We seem trapped without a cure between imperfect alternatives. Individual solutions may be our best hope. One is paradigmatic, though it depends on accidents of one's nature and circumstances: choose a vocation—parent, farmer, writer, public servant—that creates ample meanings in communities satisfying essential needs. Enjoy your work; be discreet if you realize that neighbors and friends are confused by contraries you ignore.

Notes

Introduction

1. John Stuart Mill, *On Liberty*, ed. Anne Rapaport (Indianapolis, IN: Hackett, 1978), 12.

2. Alasdair MacIntyre, *After Virtue* (Notre Dame, IN: Notre Dame University Press, 1984).

3. Mill, *On Liberty*, 12.

4. Leo F. Schnore, "Community: Theory and Research on Structure and Change," in Neil J. Smelser, ed., *Sociology: An Introduction* (New York: John Wiley, 1973), 69.

5. Amitai Etzioni, "Introduction," in *The Essential Communitarian Reader*, Amitai Etzioni, ed. (New York: Roman & Littlefield, 1998), iv.

6. Philip Selznick, *The Moral Commonwealth* (Berkeley: University of California Press,1992), 358–59.

7. Robert Nisbet, *The Quest for Community* (Wilmington, DE: ISI Books, 1981), 262.

8. Nisbet, *Quest for Community*, 261.

9. Charles Taylor, *A Secular Age* (Cambridge, MA: Harvard University Press, 2007), 2.

10. See John Stuart Mill, *Utilitarianism* (Indianapolis, IN: Hackett, 1979).

11. Aristotle, *Politics, The Basic Works of Aristotle*, ed. Richard McKeon (New York: Random House, 1941), 1253a, 1129.

12. David Weissman, *A Social Ontology* (New Haven, CT: Yale University Press, 2000).

Chapter One

1. René Descartes, *Meditations on First Philosophy: The Philosophical Writings of Descartes*, trans. John Cottingham, Robert Stoothoff, and Dugald Murdoch (Cambridge, UK: Cambridge University Press, 1984), 17.

2. Ferdinand Tönnies, *Community and Society*, trans. Charles P. Loomis (New Brunswick, NJ: Transaction, 1988), 37.

3. Tönnies, *Community and Society*, 47.

4. Tönnies, *Community and Society*, 65.

5. Selznick, *The Moral Commonwealth*, 365. Discussions of gesellschaft are familiar in democratic societies; those favorable to gemeinschaft are rare. Charles Taylor's *A Secular Age* (Cambridge, MA: Harvard University Press, 2007) is an exception, though, as its title intimates, it criticizes gesellschaft, in the manner of Tönnies, for its "narcissism," while saying less of totalizing gemeinschaft.

6. Ebenezer Howard, *Garden Cities of To-morrow* (Moscow, Russia Federation: Dodo Press, 2009).

7. See Joseph A. Schumpeter, *Capitalism, Socialism, and Democracy* (New York: Harper, 2008), 83.

8. See Friedrich Nietzsche, *On the Genealogy of Morals*, trans. Walter Kaufmann (New York: Random House, 1969).

Chapter Two

1. Tönnies, *Community and Society*, 65.

2. David Hume, *A Treatise of Human Nature*, ed. L. A. Selby-Bigge (Oxford, UK: Oxford University Press, 1978), 1.

3. David Hume, *An Inquiry Concerning Human Understanding* (Cambridge, UK: Cambridge University Press, 2007), 131–43.

4. Weissman, *A Social Ontology*, 59–60.

5. Descartes, *Meditations*, 22.

6. See Martin Luther, *Selections from his Writings* (New York: Random House, 2011).

7. Georg Simmel, *Georg Simmel: On Individuality and Social Forms* (Chicago, IL: University of Chicago Press, 1971), 324–39.

8. See Jane Jacobs, *The Death and Life of Great American Cities* (New York: Random House, 1992).

Chapter Three

1. Hume, *A Treatise of Human Nature*, 415.
2. Plato, *The Republic*, trans, F. M. Cornford (Oxford, UK: Oxford University Press, 1941), 514A–21B, 227–31.
3. Hume, *A Treatise of Human Nature*, 11.
4. William James, *The Varieties of Religious Experience* (Middletown, DE: Crossreach Publications, 2016), 1–14.
5. Karl Marx, *Communist Manifesto*, trans. Samuel Moore (Chicago, IL: Gateway Editions, 1954), 32–34.
6. Aristotle, *Metaphysics*, 1047b31–48a24, 824–25.
7. Descartes, *Meditations*, 44–48.
8. Mill, *On Liberty*, 12.
9. Mill, *Utilitarianism*, 6–10.
10. Marx, *Communist Manifesto*, 13–38.
11. Thomas Aquinas, *Summa Theologiae* (Notre Dame, IN: Christian Classics, 1989), 105–49.
12. See G. W. Leibniz, *Discourse on Metaphysics and Other Essays*, trans. Daniel Garber and Roger Ariew (Indianapolis, IN: Hackett, 1991).
13. See Joseph Fletcher, *Situation Ethics: The New Morality* (Louisville, KY: Westminster John Knox Press, 1998).
14. Mill, *On Liberty*, 12.
15. Aristotle, *Nichomachean Ethics*, 1105b25, 957.

Chapter Four

1. Descartes, *Meditations*, 17.
2. Descartes, *Meditations*, 19.
3. Mill, *On Liberty*, 9–10.
4. Descartes, *Meditations*, 17–18.
5. Jean Jacques Rousseau, *The Social Contract and Other Later Political Writings*, trans. Victor Gourevitch (Cambridge, UK: Cambridge University Press, 1997), 43.
6. Mill, *On Liberty*, xxvi.
7. Citizens United v. Federal Election Commission, 558, US 310 (2010).
8. Immanuel Kant, *Critique of Pure Reason*, trans. Norman Kemp Smith (New York: St. Martin's Press, 1929), 91–92, 103–5.

NOTES TO CHAPTER SIX

9. René Descartes, *Meditations, Meditations on First Philosophy*, trans. Elizabeth S. Haldane and G. R. S. Ross, ed. David Weissman (New Haven, CT: Yale University Press, 2026), 19. This translation uses "refuse" where Cottingham, Stoothoff, and Murdoch read "is willing, is unwilling."

10. John Locke, *Two Treatises of Government* (Cambridge, UK: Cambridge University Press, 1988), 99, 301.

Chapter Five

1. Martin Heidegger, *Nietzsche*, vol. 3, trans. Joan Stambaugh, David Farrell Krell, and Frank A. Capuzzi (San Francisco, CA: Harper, 1987), 242.

2. Heidegger, *Nietzsche*, 243.

3. Heidegger, *Nietzsche*, 243.

Chapter Six

1. W. Norris Clarke, S.J., *The One and the Many* (Notre Dame, IN: University of Notre Dame Press, 2001).

2. Selznick, *Moral Commonwealth*, 359.

3. Martin Heidegger, quotation from an unpublished manuscript of 1938, in Emmanuel Faye, "Subjectivity and Race in Heidegger's Writings," *Philosophy Today* 55, no. 3 (2011): 271–72.

4. See David Weissman, *Sensibility and the Sublime* (Berlin, Germany: Walter De Gruyter, 2016).

5. Emile Durkheim, *Suicide: A Study in Sociology* (New York: Simon and Schuster, 1951), 241–76.

6. Weissman, *A Social Ontology*, 69.

7. W. V. O. Quine, *Word and Object* (Cambridge: MIT Press, 1960), 13.

Index

affect, 52
affiliation, 11, 44, 107
  cooperation and, 115
  freedom and, 108
  temporary, 75
  virtual communities and, 26
affinities, community structure and,
    42–44
After Virtue (MacIntyre), 1, 9, 25,
    46–47, 51
agency, 22
aims, 7
alliances, 44
  gesellschaft and, 75
ambivalence, 70–76
Amish, 1
amygdala, 56
anomie, 142–143
appeals to community, 7–8
Aristotle, 9, 38–39, 49, 65, 84, 89
aspiration, 145
associations
  community structure and, 41–42
  ethos and, 43
authority, communal, 98–100
autocracy, 71
autonomy, 6–8, 22, 36, 50, 72, 89

city plasticity and, 25
communal authority and, 98–100
community and, 108
constraints and, 92–95
duty and, 95–96
free will, 103–107
irresolution and, 111–112
justice and, 100–103
obstacles to, 95–98
regions of freedom and, 90
relations and, 107
roles and, 92, 94, 107
socialization and, 90–91
socialized, 99

background, 48–50
being-in-the-truth, 15–16
beleaguered members, 27–28
beliefs, 49
  feeling and, 56
  learning, 141
Buber, Martin, 81

calculation, 8–9
care, 59–60
  community formation and, 57–58
casual communities, 45

154 INDEX

categorical imperative, 28, 37
category mistakes, 117
Catholics, 1
causal analysis, 131–132
causal language, 132
causal reciprocity, 40–41, 59, 69
change, 50–53
character, law and, 84–85
choice
  freedom of, 108
  moral identity and, 86
  of responses, 105
cities, 43, 47, 148
  conflicts of meaning and, 125
  density of, 136
  ecclesiastical, 21
  plasticity of, 25
*Citizens United v. Federal Election
  Commission*, 100–101
civil war, 128
coherence, 40
  cooperation and, 114
  decoherence, 22
  moral, 133–134
collaboration, 90–91
common interest, 26
communal authority, 98–100
communal identity, distance and, 25
communal styles, 45
communism, 73
communitarians, 4, 73, 125
communities-at-large, 3–4, 10,
  14–15, 47
  conflicts and, 122–123
  grievances and, 125
communities-of-accord, 5, 10–11,
  20–26
  cooperation and, 119
  disciplinary spaces and, 36–37

diversity and, 24–26
essential values and, 22–24
hierarchies and, 22
networks and, 21–22
communities-of-interest, 3–4, 10–14,
  148
  causes and, 40–41
  communal authority and, 99
  moral coherence and, 134
  relationships in, 59
  relative position in, 135
communities-of-meaning, 3–4,
  10–14, 148
  care and, 57
  causes and, 40–41
  communal authority and, 99
  moral coherence and, 134
  relationships in, 59
  relative position in, 135
  solidarity and, 62–63
community, 1
  appeals to, 7–8
  autonomy and, 108
  conflicts between, 122
  cooperation among, 118–119
  defining, 10
  experience of significance of, 16
  fear of costs of leaving or resisting
    demands of, 81
  form and, 39
  formation of, 8–9, 46–48, 57–59,
    115
  global, 84
  membership in, 46–48
  norms unifying, 86
  pernicious, 28–29
  resigning from, 110
  smaller-scale, 19
  socialization and, 2

INDEX 155

society as context of, 11
society as totalizing, 2
spontaneous, 15
subaltern, 4
uses of term, 3
utilitarian, 2
virtual, 26–27
community membership
conflict within, 120–121
differences in scruples among,
82
identity and, 29–30
moral orientations and, 81
personal disputes within, 120
community structure
ethos and affinities, 42–44
organizations and associations,
41–42
relations, 38–41
systems, 38
competition, 27, 50, 113–114, 123
competitive communities, 45
compromise, 82
conceptual spaces, 35
conflict, 120–129
of duty, 121–122
ideology and, 121–122
meaning and, 123–125
consequentialism, 50
constraints, 92–95
constructive thought, 126
control, 139–140
convergence, 29–31
cooperation, 113
affiliation and, 115
among communities, 118–119
communities-of-accord and, 119
gemeinschaft and, 115–116
gesellschaft and, 115–116

stability and, 114–115
among system members, 114–118
coordination, 21
core communities, 45
corporate communities, 45
cosmos, 132–133
creative destruction, 27
culture, 137–138

*The Death and Life of Great
American Cities* (Jacobs), 51
decoherence, 22
deliberation, 105–106
democracy, 96
deontology, 78
Descartes, René, 39, 51, 65, 84,
90–91, 102
determinism
hard, 103–107
soft, 106–107
development, 39
communism and, 73
Dewey, John, 8, 46, 52, 64, 67
dialectical materialism, 73
disciplinary social spaces, 4–5,
35–38
distance, communal identity and, 25
diversity, 23–26, 84, 122
Durkheim, Émile, 142
duty, 7, 70, 77–79
autonomy and, 95–96
conflicts of, 121–122
habitual responses and, 13
moral, 82
normativity and, 65
roles and, 94
to self or to social systems, 109
solidarity in gemeinschaft and, 33
Dworkin, Ronald, 9

156 INDEX

ecclesiastical cities, 21
economy, 137
effects, moral orientations and, 80–81
efficacy, 50
egoism, 109
emergence, 145
emotion, 56
  communities-of-meaning and, 12
  community formation and, 57
  fellowship and, 59–64
  meaning and, 61
the Enlightenment, 37, 50, 53, 71,
  93, 111
equal rights and opportunities, 101
essentialism, 71
ethos, community structure and,
  42–44
Etzioni, Amitai, 1
Euthyphro (Plato), 49
exclusion, 126
existentialism, 71
experience, 36
  of community's significance, 16

family, 59–60
fashion, 30
feedback, 40, 43
  normativity and, 66
feelings, 56
  family and, 59–60
  moral orientations and, 80
fellowship, 34, 38, 45
  emotion and, 59–64
final cause, 39
foreground, 48–50
form, 39
fragility, 91–92
fraternité, 36–37, 46
fraternity, 89

free will, 103–107
freedom, 1, 7, 74, 89
  affiliation and, 108
  of choice, 108
  complementary forms of, 52–53
  duty and, 70
  Mill conception of, 95–96
  regions of, 90
friendship, 12–13, 24, 47, 133
  reciprocity and, 101
frontier, 93, 119

Garden Cities of To-morrow
  (Howard), 21
gemeinschaft, 2, 16–20, 147–148
  basic needs and, 34
  beleaguered members and, 28
  communities-of-accord and, 20
  complaints and, 120
  cooperation and, 115–116
  diversity and, 24
  essential values and, 22–23
  governance and, 68–69
  hierarchy and, 22
  meaning and, 84
  moral coherence and, 133–134
  moral identity and, 83
  moral orientations and, 80
  morality and, 76–77
  networks and, 21
  obeisance and, 35
  personal differences and, 139
  religion and, 73–74
  roles and, 92
  solidarity in, 33
  subaltern communities and, 83
  tradition and, 83
  values and, 49
Genealogy of Morals (Nietzsche), 30

INDEX

157

gesellschaft, 2, 16–20, 147–148
alliances and, 75
as assembly of utilities, 33–34
atomizing effects of, 37
basic needs and, 34
beleaguered members and, 28
communities-of-accord and, 20
complaints and, 120
cooperation and, 115–116
diversity and, 24
essential values and, 22–23
governance and, 68
hierarchy and, 22
identity and, 83
justice and, 102
moral identity and, 83
moral orientations and, 80
morality and, 76–77
networks and, 21
normativity and, 75
Oneness of, 136
rationalization and, 52
roles and, 92
tolerance and, 49
values and, 48
global communities, 84
goodwill, 119
governance, normativity and, 68–69
gravitas, 60
grievances, 125

habit, 16
duty and, 13
normativity and, 65
hard determinism, 103–107
Heidegger, Martin, 126, 140
hierarchies, 22
Hobbes, Thomas, 34, 128
holism, 6, 19, 22, 146–147

holistic communities, 45
Howard, Ebenezer, 21
Hume, David, 39–40, 56, 96–97, 144

idealization, 58, 60–61, 70, 72
identity, 18
community membership and,
29–30
distance and communal, 25
gesellschaft and, 83
moral, 83–87
roles and, 50, 110
tribal, 29–30
ideology, 36, 46–47, 72–73
conflict and, 121–122
imaginary spaces, 26
immediacy, 26
imposed order, 27
individualism, 1–2, 70, 101, 139
justice and, 100
individuality, 102
Industrial Revolution, 93, 111
inhibition, 105
initiative, 37
instrumental relationships, 6, 38,
117
instrumentalities, 10, 22
interdependence, 98, 113, 116
interest. *See* communities-of-interest
interpretation, 56–57
community formation and, 57
meaning and, 61
intrinsic worth, 18

Jacobs, Jane, 51
James, William, 61, 140, 146
judgments
actions chosen and, 105
moral, 86

justice, 100–103

Kant, Immanuel, 28, 37, 51, 78–79, 81–82, 89
  on free will, 103
Kurkwille, 18
Kymlicka, Will, 9

labor, 63
language
  causal, 132
  emotion and, 56
  mechanical, 132
law
  character and, 84–85
  duty and, 78
  natural, 87–88
  stability and, 84–85
learning
  belief, 141
  socialized, 91
Leibniz, G. W., 104–105, 146
Levinas, Immanuel, 81
libertarianism, 9, 89, 93, 96
  Kant and, 79
liberté, 36
litigiousness, 118
locale, 135
locality, 45–47
Locke, John, 84, 89, 111
loyalty, 61
  community formation and, 58
  to roles, 92
Luther, Martin, 51

MacIntyre, Alasdair, 1, 9, 25, 46–47, 51
the many, 8, 131
Marx, Karl, 63, 73

meaning, 55–57. *See also* communities-of-meaning
community members bound by, 23
conflict and, 123–125
emotion and, 61
gemeinschaft and, 84
interpretation and, 61
loyalty and, 85
moral orientations and, 80
normativity and, 67–68
socialization of, 61
mechanical language, 132
Meditations (Descartes), 51, 91
memory, 106
microcommunities, 83
Mill, John Stuart, 67, 84, 100, 140
  on asocial people, 70
  autonomy and, 6, 89
  concept of freedom of, 95–96
  locality and, 46
  moral duty and, 82
  on morality, 78
  natural normativity and, 97–98
  no-harm principle, 1–2, 4, 28, 95
  politics and, 37
  regions of freedom, 90
  on social unities, 81
Monadology (Leibniz), 146
moral coherence, 133–134
moral duty, 82
moral identity, 83–87
moral judgments, 86
moral law, 51
moral orientations, 79–82
morality
  kinds of, 76–77
  Mill on, 78
  situational, 79

INDEX

multiculturalism, 14
mutual aid, 67
mutual esteem, 73

narratives
  loyalty and, 85
  unity and, 140–141
nativism, 137
natural laws, 87–88
natural normativity, 96–97
natural will, 17–18
negative feedback, 40, 66
negotiation, 8–9, 127
neighborhoods, 51–52
networks, 21–22, 44
  as constraints, 92–95
  kinds of, 92–93
Nietzsche (Heidegger), 126
Nietzsche, Friedrich, 30, 126, 146
Nisbet, Robert, 1, 5
no-harm principle, 1–2, 4, 28,
  95
normativity, 65–70
  gesellschaft and, 75
  is-must distinction and, 69–70
  moral identity and, 83
  natural, 96–97
  social, 73
norms, moral identity and, 86

obeisance, gemeinschaft and, 35
obstacles, autonomy and, 95–98
On Liberty (Mill), 6, 37, 46, 81, 89,
  97–98, 100
  concept of freedom in, 95
the One, 8, 131
  integrated or contained, 132–133
  reality testing and, 141–142
  social life and, 136

order
  imposed, 27
  rational, 87
organizations, community structure
  and, 41–42
orthodox Jews, 1

pernicious communities, 28–29
personal disputes, 120
perspective, 145–146
physical spaces, 35
Plato, 7, 28, 49, 89, 96
Platonism, 51
Plato's cave, 51, 55, 57
playing fields, 35
pluralist society, 83
politics, 37
  conflicts of meaning and, 125
Politics (Aristotle), 49
polity, 136–137
positive feedback, 40, 43, 66
power, 36
  will to, 126
predestination, 104
private spaces, 35
professional communities, 45
proscriptions, moral identity and, 86
psychological distance, 25
The Public and Its Problems
  (Dewey), 8, 52, 64
public spaces, 35
purpose, community formation and,
  58

Quine, W. V. O., 146

rational order, 87
rationalization, 51–52
reality testing, 141–142

160 INDEX

reciprocity, 6–8, 10, 12–13, 70, 84
  causal, 40–41, 59, 69
  friendship and, 101
  normativity and, 65–67
reflection, 142
relations
  Aristotle on, 39
  autonomy and, 107
  community structure and, 38–41
relationships
  as entities, 58–59
  instrumental, 6, 38, 117
  utilitarian, 12
  vocational, 45
religion, 71–72
  conflicts of meaning and, 125
  fellowship and, 60
  gemeinschaft and, 73–74
Republic (Plato), 7, 28, 49, 96
responsible members, 23
roles
  abandoning, 109–110
  autonomy and, 92, 94, 107
  duty and, 94
  gemeinschaft and, 92
  gesellschaft and, 92
  identity and, 50, 110
  loyalty to, 92
  moral orientations and, 80
Rousseau, Jean Jacques, 20, 36–37,
    63, 89, 108, 119, 140
rural *volk*, 14

sanctification, 60
Sandel, Michael, 9
satisfaction, 60
schism, 8, 11, 125
sectarianism, 125, 127
secularism, 128

self, duty to, 109
self-control, 67
self-perception, 16
self-regard, 109
self-regulation, 64
self-sufficiency, 111, 115, 131
Selznick, Philip, 1, 17–18
sensibility, 138
sentiment, 63–64
Simmel, Georg, 51
singularity, 144–145
Smith, Adam, 73
social atomism, 1, 6
social care, 37
The Social Contract (Rousseau), 20,
    36, 63, 119
social groups, 1
social life
  the One and, 136
  tension and, 25, 27
social normativity, 73
social orders, 71
social process, 73
social relations, 65
social roles, 7
social spaces, 71
  disciplinary, 35–38
social systems, 22
  diversity of, 24
  duty to, 109
  effects sustaining, 15
  structure of small, 13
social uniformity, 146
socialization, 1
  autonomy and, 89–91
  communities and, 2
  of meaning, 61
socialized autonomy, 99
socialized learning, 91

INDEX

society, 11
  communities-at-large and, 14
  disciplinary frames in, 4
  pluralist, 83
  as totalizing community, 2
soft determinism, 106–107
solidarity, 36, 61–63
  communism and, 73
space-time, 143
species, 138
spirituality, 62
spontaneity, 15
sport, 60, 123
stability, 6, 40
  character and, 84
  cooperation and, 114–115
  law and, 84–85
stabilizing routines, 85
subaltern communities, 4, 83
subjectivity, 41, 139
surrogate spaces, 26
systems
  abandoning, 109–110
  community structure and, 38
  cooperation among members of,
    114–118

Taylor, Charles, 5, 9, 37
teams, 47, 67
temporary affiliation, 75
tension, 27–29
  social life and, 25, 27
theism, 61
theology, 73–74
tolerance, 49, 83, 125
Tönnies, Ferdinand, 2, 16–18, 34,
    51, 139–140, 142
towns, 47

tradition, 83
traffic, 87, 127
tribal identity, 29–30
trust, community formation and, 58

unhappiness, 27–28
unity, narratives and, 140–141
univocity, 64
urbanity, 136
utilitarian communities, 2
utilitarian relationships, 12
Utilitarianism (Mill), 6, 37, 82, 98
utilities, 3, 7, 10, 22
  cooperation and, 117
  efficiency and, 44
  gesellschaft as assembly of, 33–34
  organizations and, 41–42
  solidarity and, 62–63
  values and, 23

values, 4, 7, 49
  community formation and, 48
  essential, 22–24
  loyalty to core, 85
Varieties of Religious Experience
    (James), 140, 146
vicarious familiarity, 26
virtual communities, 26–27
vocation
  community formation through, 12
  fellowship and, 60
vocational distance, 25
vocational relationships, 45

Wesenwille, 17
will, 17–18
  free, 103–107
  to power, 126